The Way, The Truth and The Life

Pupil's Book 5

Elizabeth Redmond &
Paul McHugh

Teachers' Enterprise in Religious Education Co. Ltd

Introduction

Welcome to *'The Way, the Truth and the Life'* Book 5. It is Jesus who tells us that he is 'the Way, the Truth and the Life' *(Jn 14:6)*.

This book is going to help you to understand that God created you and that he loves you very much.

He sends his Son, Jesus, to show us the WAY to lead a good life that will bring happiness.

You will learn about inspirational people who choose to follow Jesus in their daily life, because they know that he teaches us the TRUTH.

We know that there are times when we all fail to do what is right, but Jesus is always ready to forgive us if we are sorry and turn to him for help.

He is the one who gives us new LIFE in the sacraments - in this book we will study the Sacrament of Reconciliation. We also share in the greatest good news of all time: Jesus died on the cross, but he rose again. So through the power of his resurrection, we too can have eternal life forever with him in heaven, that is, if we choose him as our WAY, TRUTH and LIFE.

+Vincent Nichols

✠ Vincent Nichols
Archbishop of Westminster

Contents

1. Creation 4
- God is Creator 4
- Creation of Human Beings 6
- Stewards of the Earth 8
- The Fall 12
- St. Francis 16
- St. Vincent de Paul 18

2. The Commandments 20
- God Rescues His People 20
- New Improved Commandments 22
- God Sends Help 31

3. Inspirational People 34
- Inspiring Qualities 34
- Aunty Margaret....................36
- All Are Called 38
- St. Josephine Bakhita...........40
- To Be A Disciple 44
- Fr Damien 46

4. Reconciliation 48
- Please Sir!! 48
- My Actions Affect Others......50

- What is Sin? 52
- A Story of God's Love and Forgiveness 56
- Forgiveness is not Easy 58
- Sacrament of Reconciliation .60
- Going to Confession 62

5. Life in the Risen Lord....................64
- A Gift from God 64
- Jesus is with us 68
- Prayer is being with Jesus 70
- Importance of Prayer 74
- The Our Father 76
- The Rosary 78

6. People of other Faiths 80
- World Faiths 80
- Other Religions....................84
- Christianity and other Religions 86
- How should Christians relate to believers of other Faiths ..90
- Judaism and Christianity 92

Glossary 94

1. Creation

God is Creator

Know the story of Creation in Genesis and think about its meaning

One of the most famous stories in the Bible is the story of Creation in the book of Genesis. It tells us that the first way we can know about God is by looking at the world around us.

We hear how God created a **good and beautiful** world for us to enjoy.

The writer of the book of Genesis describes what happened in such a way that everyone can remember some important facts about creation.

God is Creator - the whole of creation comes from him, and depends on him.

The world is a place of goodness and blessing and God delights in it.

God said, "Let the earth produce every kind of living creature: cattle, reptiles, and every kind of wild beast... God saw that it was good." (Genesis 1:24-25)

We can understand quite a lot about nature, describe how nature works and even learn to have some control over it.

But we don't fully understand how everything came into existence or how God is present in the world in mysterious ways.

We know that God is creator, but we don't fully understand how he made everything come into existence.

The story of Creation can be found in Gen 1-31, and Gen 2:5-25.

Activities

1. God had many reasons for creating the world. Here are two of them: **to provide things we need** and to **provide things we enjoy**.

   (a) Copy the box diagram into your book. Underneath each heading, list some of the things God gave us. Some things may go into more than one box.

GOD'S GIFTS	
Things we need	**Things we enjoy**

   (b) Choose one thing from your list and say what makes it good.

   (c) If one thing from creation were to disappear, what would you miss most?

2. (a) Describe something you have made in as much detail as possible.

   (b) In what way were you using the gifts that God has given to you, for example, your eyes, hands etc.?

   (c) What material from God's creation did you use?

   (d) How did you feel when you had completed your creation?

3. Choose something in nature that speaks to you about God, for example: stars at night, setting sun, trees in a park.
   Write a poem or prayer to thank God for it.

4. (a) If you could ask God three questions about his creation, what would they be?

   (b) Now that you know the story of Creation, what do you think God's answer to one of your questions would be?

Creation of Human Beings

Know why God made us

In the book of Genesis we are told that humanity was the greatest act of God's creation.

Then God said, *"Let us make man in our own image, in the likeness of ourselves, and let them be masters of the fish of the sea, the birds of heaven, the cattle, all the wild beasts and all the reptiles that crawl upon the earth."* (Genesis 1:26)

First important message: God made us so that we can know, love and serve him here on earth and be happy with him forever in heaven.

Second important message: We are created in the image and likeness of God. God has created us with a body and an immortal soul: so that we are both *physical* and *spiritual*.

When people look at us they should be able to see something of God in us by the way we show love and concern for one another.

We can think for ourselves. We can form relationships with others and with God. We too can create things.

*"It was you who created my inmost self, and put me together
in my mother's womb;
for all these mysteries I thank you:
for the wonder of myself,
for the wonder of your works."*
(Psalm 139:13-14)

TRUTHS ABOUT GOD

God created everything.

God saw that all creation was good.

God made mankind in his own image and likeness.

We believe that the Bible tells us **WHY** God created the world, but it does not tell us **HOW** he created it.

We know that creation began with God and continues to belong to him.

Activities

1. **(a)** Make a list of the ways in which human beings are different from animals.

   (b) List three things we have in common with animals.

2. Work in Groups.
   (a) Write down the names of the gifts and skills of each person in the group, for example, kindness, thoughtfulness, the ability to sing, play sport, play a musical instrument etc.

   (b) Make a collage, or flags of the gifts of each person in your group.

   (c) As a whole class, plan a liturgical celebration to thank God for these gifts.

   - Write your own bidding prayers to thank God for all his gifts to us.

   - Bring in to class something you are proud of, a piece of school-work or a prize etc.

   - Choose an appropriate song or hymn of thanks to God.

   - Decide when the best time would be to have this celebration.

3. Create a character profile of a person whom you think reflects some of the qualities of God.

Word Box

womb
mysteries
image and likeness of...
spiritual
immortal soul
bidding prayers

Clues -
concerned about others
brave
wants to be the best
kind
selfish
courageous
produces good things
truthful
proud
thinks of others
accepts responsibility
show-off
grumpy
never shares

7

Stewards of the Earth

Know that God calls us to care for creation

We know that God made us in his own image. Another important message in the story of creation in Genesis is that **God wants us to be stewards of creation.** This means that we have to use our gifts and talents to care for the whole world and other people. We get our food from plants and animals, but we also have to care for them.

God blessed them, saying: "Be fruitful, multiply and fill the earth and subdue it; and have dominion over the fish of the sea, the birds of the air and every living thing that moves upon the earth." (Gen. 1:28 RSV)

We have been made responsible for looking after the earth for God. He wants us to enjoy it but not to abuse it. God made us caretakers or stewards of Creation. We do not own the world; we are simply looking after it.

This is a big responsibility and it means we not only have to take care of ourselves, but we must look after other people and all of creation.

God has given each one of us many talents so that we can share in his creative life.

Michelangelo paints the Sistine Chapel

Human beings, from earliest times, have made music, painted pictures, built extraordinary things and made great discoveries.

Isaac Newton discovers gravity

We have also been able, through using our gifts, to make medicines, and learn to cultivate crops and farm animals.

We make clothes to protect ourselves, and build homes to live in.

There are times when we fail to be good stewards of Creation

We know that in our world there are people who are fortunate and others who go hungry.

Sin entered the world because human beings disobeyed God's plan.
In a mysterious way we suffer from the result of this: we have to constantly make an effort to be unselfish and to think of the needs of others.

Unfortunately, there are people who want to build up their own power and wealth; they don't care about others.

Because of this, they cause enormous suffering.

When we watch the news on television, we see examples of war, famine, disease and lots of innocent people in great difficulty.

9

No matter where we live, we can choose to be a **co-creator** or a **de-creator**.

A **co-creator** wants to build up God's world.

A **de-creator** has chosen to act selfishly or thoughtlessly.

Look at the examples below.

Co-creators vs. De-creators

Activities

1. Read pages 8-9 again.

   Design a notice for the school Notice Board with the title:

   'Stewards of Creation'.

   Use bullet points to list all the things we should do in order to be good stewards.

   If you wish, you can also use pictures as well.

2. Look at the pictures of the **co-creators** shown on this page.

   Describe some of the activities that show how the **co-creators** are making good use of their gifts.

Word Box

dominion   steward

subdue   abuse

Activities

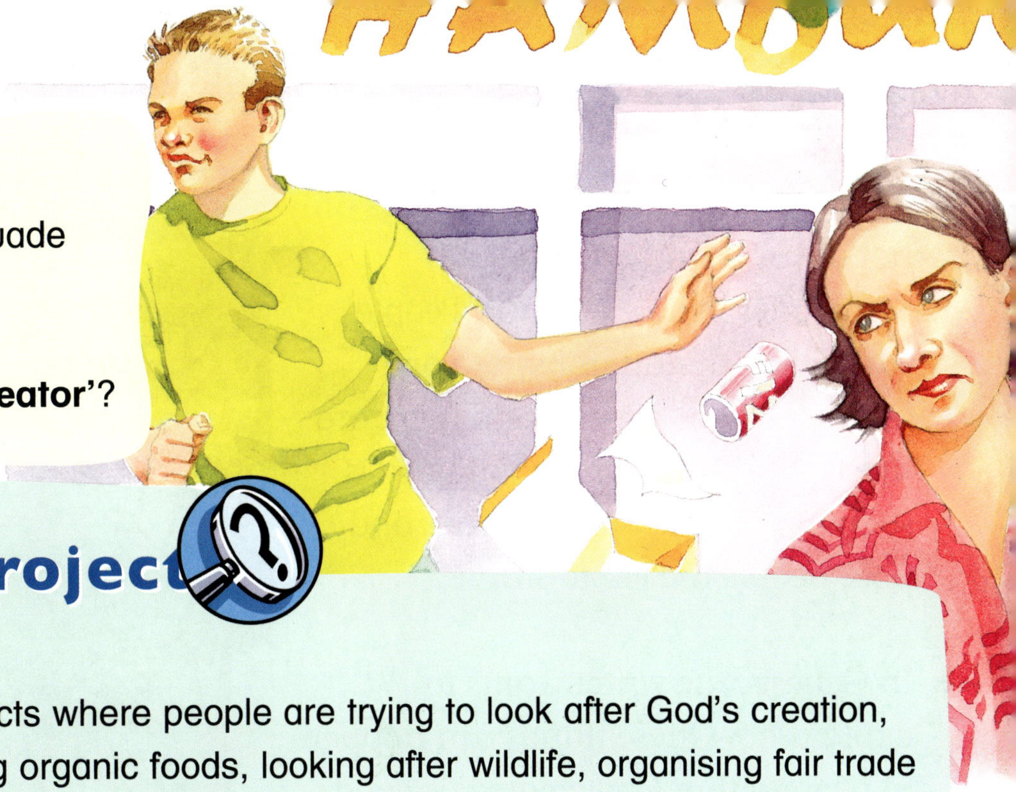

3. How could you persuade someone who is a **'de-creator'**...

    ...to become a **'co-creator'**?

Research Project

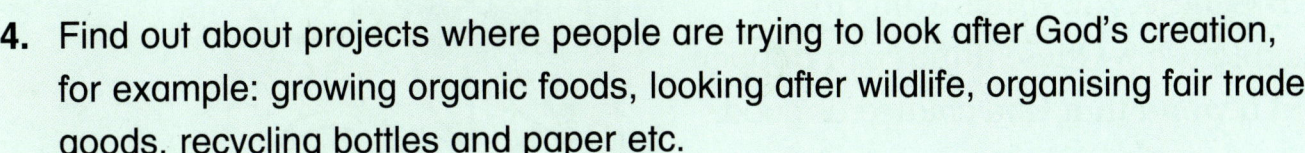

4. Find out about projects where people are trying to look after God's creation, for example: growing organic foods, looking after wildlife, organising fair trade goods, recycling bottles and paper etc.

    Choose one and explain what is happening and why this is helping to take care of God's creation.

 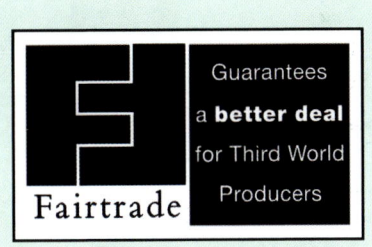 

5. Research the life of a famous scientist, musician or artist who could be described as a co-creator with God.

    (a) Write a few lines to explain who the person is.

    (b) Give some information about how the person's work has contributed to the lives of others.

The Fall

Know and reflect on the story of the Fall

We know that in our world things are not always good and happy. Sometimes people get hurt. People can be selfish and unkind to one another. In the wider world there are unjust things happening, money is spent on unnecessary luxuries and poor people are left to starve.

In Genesis, the writer wants to explain how these things can happen in a world that God created as good.

Chapter 3 of the book of Genesis tells the story of how things began to go wrong. It helps us to understand how, through the actions of human beings, good things can go wrong.
The writer describes Adam and Eve living in a beautiful garden to show that they had a special gift of friendship with God. God told them that they could eat any fruit except the fruit on the tree in the middle of the garden. God said: "You must not eat it, nor touch it, under pain of death."

However, the serpent came and told Eve that if she ate that fruit she would know about good and evil like God. Until then she had only known about good.

"You must not eat it, nor touch it, under pain of death." (Gen. 3.3)

12

So Eve disobeyed God. She ate the fruit and gave some to Adam.

Immediately, they knew they had done wrong; they had lost the special gift of friendship with God for themselves and for all their descendants.

So they tried to hide from God. God, who knows all things, knew what they had done.

He told them that they would have to leave the garden, because they had disobeyed him.

Their lives would no longer be easy, they would have to work hard to get food and eventually they would die.

THIS STORY SHOWS US THAT...

God has given us freedom:-
- to choose to do things,
- to love him and each other,
- to think about things,
- to form our own opinions.

This freedom was misused:-
- the first man and woman disobeyed God,
- they committed the first sin, known as original sin,
- because of their disobedience friendship with God was lost.

Adam and Eve are banished from the Garden of Eden.

Original Sin

This first sin is called **original sin** because it was committed at the origin of the human race.

We are all affected by it, because we are all members of the human race.

Through original sin we lost the special friendship with God, which was **original grace**.

Nothing could ever be the same again for anyone.

THIS STORY HELPS US TO…

Understand things about our lives today

- It tells us about our feelings of envy, the desire to dominate others or to 'get even' when things go wrong.

- It helps us to see why sometimes we fail to do good and instead are selfish and unkind.

We know now that this evil is not from God; it is the result of the first act of disobedience and selfishness by our first parents.

Fortunately, this is just the beginning of our history.

The Bible goes on to explain how God works in wonderful ways to restore our friendship with him!

Activities

1. Look at the illustrations below and draw your own circles with **God** written in one and **Me** in the other.

   (a) In the first circle write down the gifts God has given you.

   (b) In the second circle write down what you can do for God using your special gifts.

   (c) What do you think is the most precious thing God has given you? Why?

   (d) What do you think is the most important thing you can do for God? Why?

2. (a) Think about the story of Adam and Eve. Think of times when making a wrong choice has spoilt things for you and others: **at home, at school, playing with friends**

   (b) Describe what happened.

   (c) How did it make you feel?

   (d) How did it make others feel?

   (e) What would you do if you were in that same situation today?

3. As a class, plan a Service of Reconciliation to ask God's forgiveness for the things we have done wrong.

   (a) Work in small groups to decide on bidding prayers to ask for:

   (i) God's forgiveness for...

   (ii) his help for our families and for those suffering in the world.

   (b) Choose a hymn or song.

Word Box

original sin   dominate

original grace   desire

St. Francis

Know about individuals who inspire us to respect creation

St. Francis loved nature and had a great love of animals. He treated all living things with respect because they were God's creation.

He even called the sun and the moon his brother and sister. He saw the fingerprint of God in every leaf.

One day Francis went to preach in a small town in the north of Italy.

When he arrived, the people were too worried to listen to him because they were being terrorised by a wolf, which was living outside the walls of the town.

No one left the town unless they were in large groups or armed! Francis listened as the people explained that the wolf had eaten their lambs and threatened their children.
No one felt safe.

"Show me where the monster lives," said Francis. He placed his trust in God and he set off to find the wolf. The crowds set out with him. Suddenly, the wolf sprang out and growled fiercely.

Francis looked straight at the wolf. "Come closer," he said and he made the sign of the cross over the snarling animal. "In the name of Jesus I command you not to hurt me or anyone else again." At these words the wolf closed its gaping jaws and lay down at Francis' feet.

16

Then Francis scolded the wolf. "You have been behaving very badly, even killing people. If you promise to behave yourself I will make sure you are never chased again, and that you have food to eat, because I know it is hunger which has made you behave badly.

"Do I have your promise?"

The wolf looked up as if to agree and followed Francis back into the town.

A large crowd gathered to see the amazing sight of the wolf trotting meekly beside him.

Activities

1. Read the story of Francis again.

   (a) Francis intended preaching to the people - what made him change his mind?

   (b) Draw a symbol for Francis that would show his love for creation.

2. Imagine Francis is coming to your school or town.
   What would you do to show him some things you think he would enjoy.

3. Read the Canticle of Francis.
   Use it as a model to inspire you to write your own song about creation.

Research

4. Find out about Francis preaching to the birds and write a story about it.
   Or, find out about St. Martin de Porres, or St. Philip Neri.

Worksheet for Activity 3

Canticle of St. Francis - Photocopiable work sheet 59 (Teacher Book)

St. Vincent de Paul

Know about people who look after the vulnerable members of society

God has given all of us the ability to bring joy and happiness into the world. But we can easily hurt each other. We are all vulnerable in different ways. Some people are vulnerable because they are more easily hurt than others, some because they are physically or mentally sick and others because they are homeless or refugees.

Vincent de Paul

Vincent came from a poor farming family. Because he was very bright, his parents made many sacrifices to give him a proper education. After leaving school he became a priest.

At first, life was very comfortable for Vincent. Then one day, he visited a dying man who wanted to receive the Sacrament of Reconciliation. Vincent was shocked at the poverty of this poor, old, frail figure. It was a visit that was to change his whole life.

At that time, many people in France were poor and hungry. They did not know God, because no one had taken the time to tell them. Vincent spent his time comforting and supporting the poor and sick. He showed them the love of God through the acts of kindness he performed and by celebrating the sacraments with them. He lived by the commandment to "love your neighbour as yourself."

Vincent helped homeless children, whom he found wandering on the streets. He set up groups in churches to help the poor and to visit the sick.

He believed that by serving these people he was serving Jesus. He reached out to them all with a great love. His work took him into the poorest of homes, prisons and workhouses. He treated everyone with the same love and compassion.

Many young men were attracted to Vincent's work and life of service.

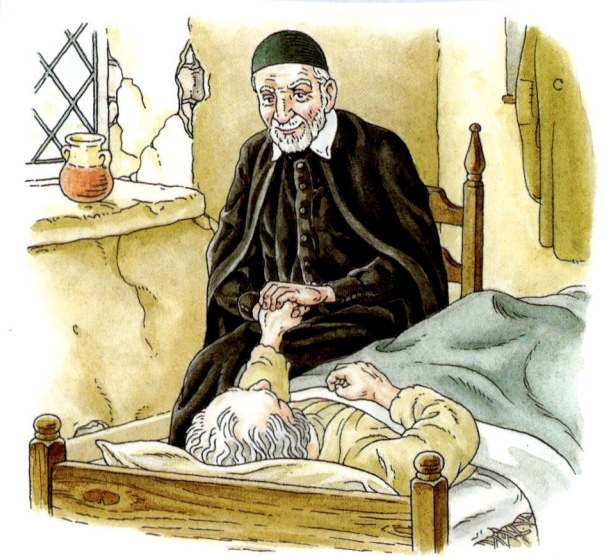

Vincent was eventually canonized and is known as St. Vincent de Paul. There are many parishes all over the world with a Vincent de Paul Society to carry on his work.

Activities

1. Write down three things that you think show how Vincent cared for the vulnerable people in society.

Research Project

2. Choose one of the following groups and find out how they help the weakest members of society:

- Missionaries of Charity founded by Mother Teresa of Calcutta

- St. Vincent de Paul Society

- Little Sisters of the Poor

- Sisters of Nazareth

- L'Arche Communities founded by Jean Vanier

- CAFOD

3. Make a postcard presentation of the Key Points of your research to share with the class.

4. What have you learnt from your research about how the vulnerable should be treated?

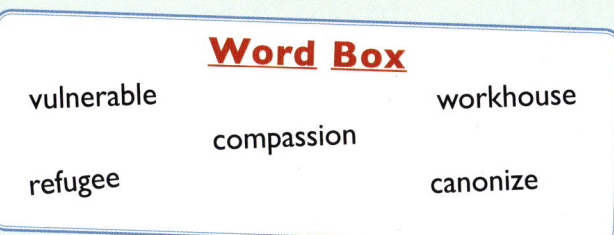

Word Box

vulnerable   workhouse
      compassion
refugee   canonize

2. The Commandments

God Rescues His People

Know and appreciate the purpose of the Ten Commandments

Many years ago, long before Jesus was born, God's people lived in Egypt. They were badly treated there, but worse than that, they had started to forget about God. They had even begun to worship some of the Egyptian gods - statues of animals and other creatures. It was time for God to rescue them.

God called Moses to persuade Pharaoh, the king of Egypt, to let the people go and, after many troubles, Moses led his people out into the desert, where God watched over them. But their troubles weren't over by a long way. The people grumbled about the hard life in the desert. Some of them even said to Moses, "Why did you bring us out of Egypt? We had plenty to eat and drink there. We are hungry and thirsty here in the desert!" But God loved his people very much and he provided food and water for them.

When the people had food and water, God spoke to Moses on Mount Sinai...

"I will make a covenant with the people," he said. "You have seen how I have led you out of Egypt and brought you here and looked after you. I want these people to be my own. Go and ask the people if they will listen to me and obey me."

Moses went and asked the people and they agreed. "All that the Lord has spoken, we will do," they said.

So God and the people made a **covenant** – a promise to love and belong to each other – and God gave Moses some commandments to help the people stay close to him. Here they are:

The Ten Commandments

1. I am the Lord your God. You shall have no other gods before me.
2. You shall not use the name of the Lord your God wrongly (in vain).
3. Remember to keep the Lord's Day holy.
4. Honour your father and your mother.
5. You shall not kill.
6. You shall not be unfaithful in marriage (commit adultery).
7. You shall not steal.
8. You shall not tell lies (bear false witness) about your neighbour.
9. You shall not be envious of (covet) your neighbour's wife.
10. You shall not be envious of (covet) your neighbour's belongings. (Exodus 20:1-17)

Activities

1. Write down the following words and choose the correct meaning from the box to put with each word. You may use the glossary at the back of this book to help you.
   - Honour
   - Adultery
   - Covet
   - Bear false witness

   - To be unfaithful in marriage
   - To lie (especially in public)
   - To show respect and love for
   - To be jealous and angry about what someone else has

2. Which of these commandments are about loving God, and which are about loving other people? Make two boxes. Write GOD in one and PEOPLE in the other. Now put the number of the commandments into each box - for example, number 2 goes into the box marked GOD.

3. Look at the first commandment. How do you think people of your own age might fail to keep this commandment?

4. Work in groups. Choose one of the Ten Commandments. Dramatise how you would keep it and see if the rest of the class can work out which one it is.

New Improved Commandments

> Understand that the Commandments are a gift from God to help us

We are now going to journey in our imagination to another planet, where people think that the Ten Commandments given to Moses many, many years ago are out of date and they want to see how they can update them.

THE TIME: 2433 AD

THE PLACE: Elysium, a pleasant planet warmed by a star.

THE SITUATION: We know that there are many colonies in space. Elysium has been identified as an ideal place for a new colony.

A hundred thousand people are transported there in a fleet of giant space cruisers.

THE LEADERS: Zena and Zen are leaders of the High Council of Elysium. They are responsible for approving what laws to follow.

They are also responsible for making sure people keep those laws. They call their first meeting of the High Council.

22

First High Council Meeting

It is decided that the Old Commandments are out of date. The language seems strange. So the High Council decides that the people of Elysium will only follow rules based on the old commandments 4-10.

Here are some of the things the Council members said:

Second High Council Meeting

Very soon a Second High Council was called to discuss changes to the rules 4-10.

Many in the Council felt that since it was your friends that mattered most in life, then the rules should be about them. So Zena and Zen agree to a new version of the rules being tried for one month.

Leave out the first 3 commandments. Why bring God into it?

Old Commandments

4. Honour your father and mother.
5. You shall not kill.
6. You shall not commit adultery.
7. You shall not steal.
8. You shall not bear false witness against your neighbour.
9. You shall not covet your neighbour's wife.
10. You shall not covet your neighbour's goods.

Yes, let's work on the old commandments 4-10. At least they make sense.

New Rules: Version 1

4. **Respect your father and your mother** ... only if you get along with them.
5. **You shall not kill (hurt, harm)** ... your friends.
6. **You shall not be unfaithful in marriage** ... when it might hurt a friend of yours.
7. **You shall not steal** ... from a friend.
8. **You shall not tell lies about your neighbour** ... when he or she is a friend.
9. **You shall not be jealous about someone's wife or husband** ... when it involves a friend.
10. **You shall not be jealous about what someone has** ... if he or she is a friend of yours.

Here are some of the headlines in the Elysium's newspapers for that first month.

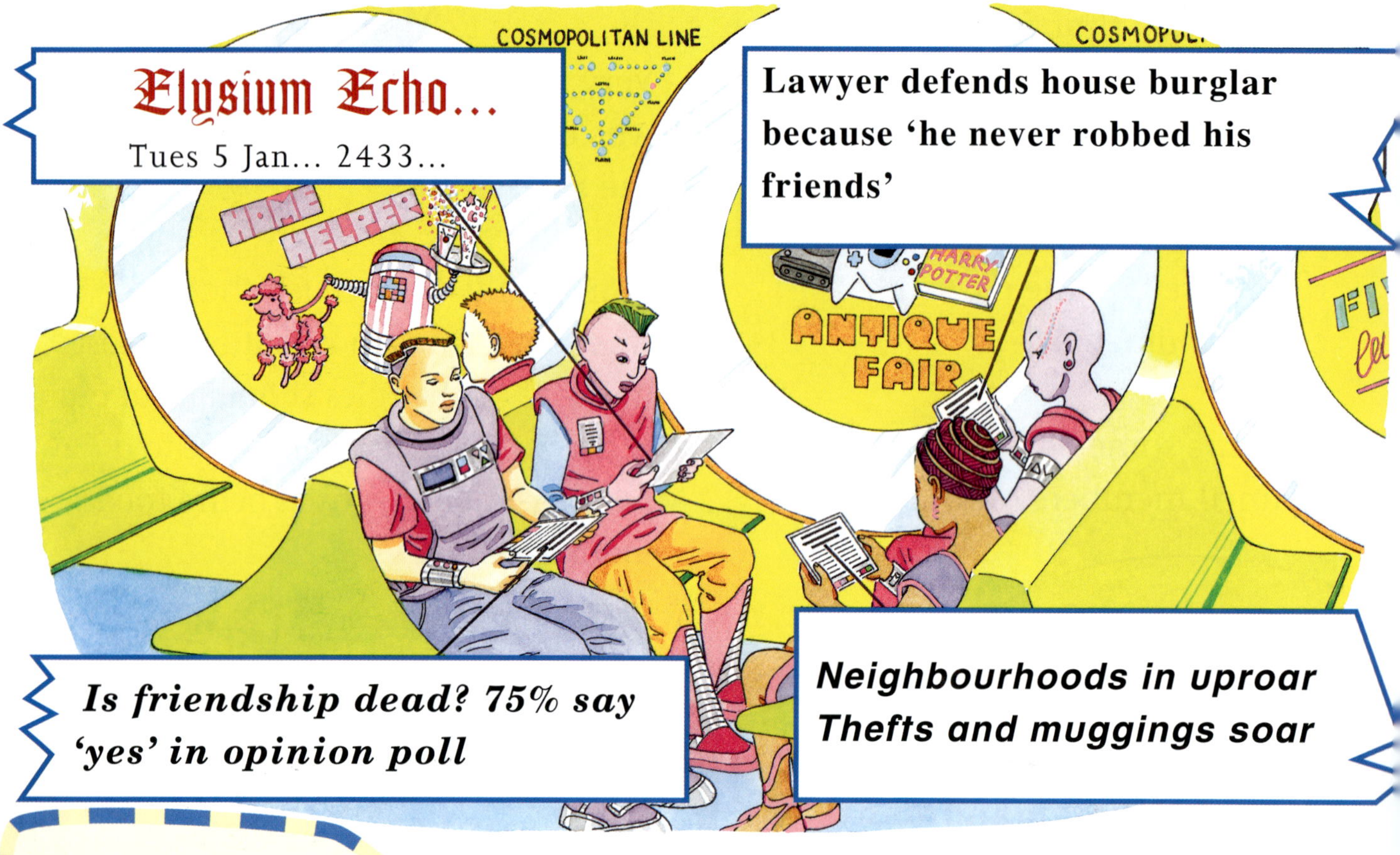
Elysium Echo...
Tues 5 Jan... 2433...
COSMOPOLITAN LINE
Lawyer defends house burglar because 'he never robbed his friends'
HOME HELPER
ANTIQUE FAIR
HARRY POTTER
Is friendship dead? 75% say 'yes' in opinion poll
Neighbourhoods in uproar
Thefts and muggings soar

Activities

1. Work in pairs.

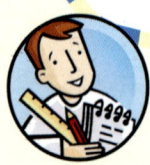

Discuss the new rules Version 1. Do you think they are going to work?

(a) Make a list of the reasons why you think they **will work.**

(b) Make a list of the reasons why you think they **will not work**.

2. Someone in the High Council tries (halfway through the month) to **'fix'** the new rules by making a law that everyone should be friends with everyone else. Do you think this law could work?

Give reasons for your answer.

Third High Council Meeting

One month later a Third High Council was called. The 'New Rules: Version 1' had been a disaster. Everyone realised that whether someone was your friend or not should not be the reason for changing rules.

Still, many in the Council felt that it was harsh to follow the rules as 'hard and fast' rules, that is, rules you 'must' keep.

Why not think of them as 'guidelines' to follow when it suited you? So Zena and Zen agreed to a second new version of the rules being tried for one month.

New Rules: Version 2

4. **Respect your father and your mother** … only when it suits you.

5. **You shall not kill** … unless it does more good than harm to kill.

6. **You shall not be unfaithful in marriage** … unless it doesn't harm anyone.

7. **You shall not steal** … unless it doesn't harm anyone.

8. **You shall not tell lies about your neighbour** … unless it doesn't harm anyone.

9. **You shall not be jealous about someone's wife or husband** … unless it doesn't harm anyone.

10. **You shall not be jealous about what someone has** … unless it doesn't harm anyone.

Activities

Elysium Echo…
Friday 5 Feb - 2433

'I was harming no one', girl shoplifter (14) claims…

1. Look at the headline in the Elysium Echo for 5 February.

   Do you think the girl was keeping the 'Version 2' rule about stealing?

   Explain why or why not?

Word Box

adultery   covenant
false witness   Ten Commandments

Activities

2. Version 1 was a disaster. Will 'New Rules: Version 2' work any better?

Explain why or why not.

Elysium Echo
Tuesday 9 Feb 2433

…Thefts and muggings still go up…

… Prisons are emptying survey shows

… High Council to call crisis meeting…

…'Temptation to steal exam papers too hard to resist' cheating student claims!

3. If you were the Head of the cheating student's school, would you accept his excuse and let him off?

Why or why not?

4. 'Doing the right thing all the time must hurt some of the time.'

Do you agree or disagree?

Explain.

Word Box

Honour   Lord's Day   respect   covet

Fourth High Council Meeting

One month later a Fourth High Council was called. The 'New Rules: Version 2' had also been a disaster. Everyone realised that some basic rules had to be followed strictly - otherwise there would be chaos.

Everyone in the High Council was squabbling. They were arguing about yet another twist to the rules. Zena and Zen lost patience. They spoke to the High Council:

Ladies and Gentlemen of the High Council, we have listened each month to a different version of the old laws. Each month we have seen our fair land of Elysium torn apart by violence and disrespect. We now know that the law:

1. *Must apply to friends and strangers alike.*

2. *Must be followed whether it suits you or not.*

3. *Must be followed whether it is easy or not.*

So Zena and Zen put forward a third new version of the rules, to be tried for a month.

New Rules: Version 3

4. **Respect your father and your mother** ~~only~~ ... no ifs or buts.

5. **You shall not kill** ... no ifs or buts.

6. **You shall not be unfaithful in marriage** ... no ifs or buts.

7. **You shall not steal** ... no ifs or buts.

8. **You shall not tell lies about your neighbour** ... no ifs or buts.

9. **You shall not be jealous about someone's wife or husband** ... no ifs or buts.

10. **You shall not be jealous about what someone has** ... no ifs or buts.

Activities

Work in Groups.

1. **(a)** Read all the questions below sent to the High Council Advisory Service (HCAS).

From: Police
To: HCAS
We are holding a man who viciously mugged another man. He said he has not broken any rule since the man he mugged is not dead.
What should we do?

From: Zelda (16)
To: HCAS
My mother says I'm not respecting her.

I don't answer her back. I just don't answer her.

I am not breaking the rules so what is her problem?

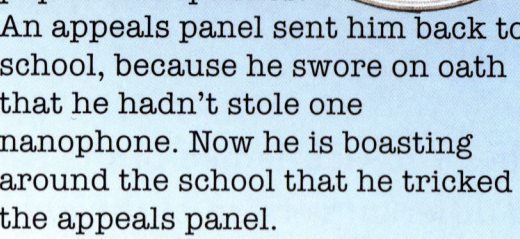

From: Head of School 1V
To: HCAS
We recently expelled a boy for stealing pupils' nanophones. An appeals panel sent him back to school, because he swore on oath that he hadn't stole one nanophone. Now he is boasting around the school that he tricked the appeals panel.
He said that because he's stolen many nanophones, he could swear solemnly that he had not stolen (just) one. He also says he has not broken any rules since he did not lie. This is causing us major headaches. Please help us out.

(b) What advice would you give to the Police?

(c) What advice would you give to the Head of School 1V?

(d) What would you say to Zelda to help her understand that what she is doing is wrong?

2. Write down what you think about the following:
   (a) Is giving a false impression the same a telling a lie?
   (b) Is borrowing without telling the same as stealing?
   (b) Is failing to do good the same as doing bad?

Fifth High Council Meeting

One month later, a Fifth High Council was called. The 'New Rules: Version 3' had not worked out as well as Zena and Zen had hoped.

In despair, they asked for any suggestions. For once, no one in the High Council spoke. Then an old lady rose slowly and spoke...

Ladies and Gentlemen, we have followed different rules for four months now and we have no peace. We must go back to the Ten Commandments. We must look to the One who gave us these Commandments and understand WHY he gave them to us. This is the One who wrote a law in our minds and hearts. This One is God and we have forgotten him. We have put aside three of the commandments and tried to change the rest. I suggest we all return to the Ten Rules God gave. They have been successful for three thousand years - whilst our efforts could not even last for three months.

There was a big round of applause and everyone agreed. Because at last they understood that the problem is not with the commandments, but with us. Without God's help we are unable to keep them.

Activities

1. The New Rules: Version 4 (see below) looks familiar. Where have you seen it before?

2. Link each commandment with a meaning given beside.

New Rules: Version 4

1. I am the Lord your God. You shall not have strange gods before me.
2. You shall not take the name of the Lord your God in vain.
3. Remember to keep holy the Lord's Day.
4. Honour your father and mother.
5. You shall not kill.
6. You shall not commit adultery.
7. You shall not steal.
8. You shall not bear false witness against your neighbour.
9. You shall not covet your neighbour's wife.
10. You shall not covet your neighbour's goods.

- Do not take what is not yours to take. Do not be lazy and depend on the hard work of others.
- Do not be jealous in your heart about what another person has.
- Do not lie or try to give a false impression to someone else.
- Set aside time for God and each other in the business of your lives.
- Put God first. Don't let anything else come between you and God.
- God, God's name and all the things of God are holy. Remember this and show respect.
- Do not harm the innocent in any way whatsoever.
- Be faithful in marriage. Learn to say no to yourself when it is right to do so.
- Do not be jealous in your heart about the close relationships and friendships of others.
- Treat your parents and all who have helped guide you with kindness, care and thankfulness.

God Sends Help

Reflect on the birth of Jesus

We now return to Earth to reflect on how God sent his only Son, Jesus, into the world. Later on, we will see how Jesus teaches us to live the commandments and how he gives us the help we need to do so.

Let's imagine that our spaceship gently descends towards Earth. It also goes back in time over 2,000 years so that we can think about what the birth of Jesus really means for us.

As we get closer, a star appears. It is shining very brightly and almost seems to highlight the entrance to a cave. The air is very still and the night seems strangely silent and holy. As we hover outside the entrance, a familiar scene appears inside.

A young woman, tired but happy, is stooping over a cattle-feeding trough filled with hay. In her arms is a tiny, newborn baby, wrapped in white cloth. Bending to help her is an older man, her husband.

In the corners of the cave, a couple of donkeys and a pair of oxen look on. The oxen move slightly but they make no sound.

31

God fulfills his promise

We know that this small, helpless baby is God himself who has come to live with us as a human being.

Why did he come like this, so small and weak?

The first people chose not to obey God, and so the relationship between God and people was broken. But that didn't mean God stopped loving us - his children. God loves us very much and so he would not let things stay like that.

From the very beginning he had planned a way to save us so that we could come to know him and love him and be happy with him.

This is what we are remembering when we celebrate Christmas.

God loved us so much that he sent his Son into our world as a tiny baby - to live with us and be totally dependent on human beings for everything he needed.

> The word we use for this is INCARNATION. This means God, who is a spirit, took human flesh and blood and became a real man.

When we look at the Christmas crib we remember how much God loves us.

Whenever we see a tiny baby in its mother's lap or being carried lovingly in its father's arms, we can think of how God loves us and cares for us, and how he came himself as a baby needing love and care to show us how to trust completely.

God became a human being so that human beings could come back to God.

Activities

1. If someone asked you why Christians celebrate Christmas, how would you explain it to them?

2. Imagine you could leave that spaceship and go into the cave at Bethlehem.

   Write a 'senses poem' or a story to describe what you experience.

   What would you... *See, Hear, Smell, Touch and what would you feel inside?*

3. Prepare a liturgy to celebrate the Incarnation, using this plan.

   - Choose a Christmas Carol.

   - A reading from the Gospel of Luke.

   - Bidding Prayers.

   - A carol to finish with.

Word Box

incarnation

3. Inspirational People

Inspiring Qualities

Reflect on what it means to be an inspirational person

An inspirational person is someone whose words or actions challenge us to reflect on our own lives. We may even change something we do or the way we behave because of the example they give us.

These inspirational people may be ordinary or talented. They may be very thoughtful and kind towards others. They may have overcome some great difficulty in their own lives.

Or they may have achieved something outstanding through their determination and courage.

Such people may inspire us to be courageous or help us to overcome obstacles and to do our best in everything we undertake.

We may know of people who have had a very hard life. But instead of thinking of their misfortune, they think of all the good things they can do. They work hard to make the best of every situation.

Some of these people are well known, like those in the photographs, but there may be others who live and work among us. They are an inspiration to us because they show us what can be done if we are courageous and stand up for what we believe. They know that with God's help they can achieve their goals. Some of them live their lives totally for God and others. The Church recognises that they are saints.

Activities

1. Your teacher will give you a copy of this design, or you can use a computer to produce it yourself.

    (a) Under each star write one thing that would make a person inspirational.

    (b) On top of each star write the name of a person you know who possesses these qualities.

    (c) Which of these qualities do you admire most? Why?

2. Making a Difference. Imagine yourself in ten years time.

    Describe one thing you would like to do that would make the world a better place for others.

Worksheet for Activity 1

'Stars' - Photocopiable work sheet 62
(Teacher book)

Aunty Margaret

by Paul (12 years old)

Here is a true story of a person who dedicates her life to helping others.

Aunty Margaret has three children and has been married for 24 years to Martin. Everybody likes to visit her because she makes you feel so welcome and always seems interested in everything and everyone.

One day, I went to see her. I needed someone to talk to because I had just failed three of my exams.

When I walked in, Aunty Margaret greeted me with a cup of tea saying, "You look as though you could do with this." We were just about to tackle the reason for my visit when a dull groan came from next door. She went quickly to the living room. I followed her, to see what was wrong.

Uncle Martin has a serious disease which affects all his muscles. This has developed slowly over the last five years and he is now unable to do very much for himself. I felt awkward as I stood in the doorway watching my aunt clearing up the mess he had made, while she gently chatted to him.

It was almost an hour before we were able to continue our conversation in the kitchen. I would happily have forgotten it, as it no longer seemed important, but Aunty Margaret insisted I told her what was troubling me.

Half an hour passed, and I was now feeling much better; failing exams was not the worst thing that could happen. I was about to say good-bye when a car horn sounded outside.

It was half-five and my cousin Simon was returning from school. Quickly, Aunty Margaret and I went outside to see her youngest son descending the ramps of the school minibus. Simon had been involved in a "hit and run" accident last year, and was paralysed from the waist down. He had also suffered some brain damage which had affected his speech.

Many times Simon and I had got into mischief when we were younger. Once we had been 'grounded' for three weeks for skipping school and going to the fair! His accident was a great shock to us all, and to be honest, it was very difficult for me to see my wild cousin in a wheelchair!!

I don't know how my aunt managed to cope with Simon who could do nothing at all for himself. Yet, when I saw the joy on his face as he returned home to his mum and the love and attention she gave him, I felt ashamed because I was embarrassed by his disability.

Every day, Aunty Margaret looks after her husband and son, as well as many other people like me who call in for a chat! I often wonder how she can be so full of compassion and good humour.

I have never asked her about how she copes, or what she feels, but I know that she has a deep friendship with Jesus and she draws her strength from him. There are very few times in the week when she leaves the house, but she will go to daily Mass and she brings Holy Communion to Martin and Simon on Sundays.

Aunty Margaret's kindness and generosity show that she wants to live her life as Jesus taught us. By doing that, she finds inner peace and comfort.

Activities

1. **(a)** Make a medal or a star with Aunty Margaret's name on it.

   (b) Write a certificate to go with it saying why she was given this award.

2. Aunty Margaret had a deep friendship with Jesus, which clearly gives her strength. What do you do in a difficult situation in order to find strength?

All Are Called

Know what it means to be a follower of Jesus

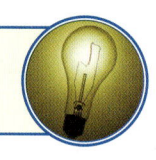

At our Baptism we receive the grace to follow Jesus. This is like receiving a little light inside us to guide us on the right path, the way of truth and love. Each day, we have to ask Jesus to make that light grow within us, so that we will become people of great courage and generosity.

When the disciples wanted to be followers of Jesus they asked him what they had to do. Jesus taught them the greatest commandment:

Love the Lord your God with all your heart, soul and mind and love your neighbour as yourself.

Then, on another occasion he explained in more detail what was necessary:

If anyone wants to be a follower of mine he must deny himself, take up his cross daily and follow me.
(Luke 9:23)

To deny yourself means that, out of love, you willingly give up your right to do what you want and instead do what God wants.

Be compassionate!
Do not judge!
Pray for those who treat you badly!

These words are tough. They are not for those seeking an easy life, but for those who want to live life to the full. Jesus wants each person to be aware of all their gifts and talents and then to be willing to use them to help others, not just to keep them for themselves. When a person chooses to live like this and puts their trust in Jesus to help, then that person will experience deep inner peace and strength, even in times of difficulties. They will also bring great joy to others.

Activities

1. When we accept difficulties, we take up our cross, like Jesus did.

   (a) Make a large cardboard cross.

   (b) Stick on pictures or words that reflect some of the difficulties people may have to face in life.

   (c) Around the cross, put words and pictures to show the way we can get help from Jesus.

2. Read **Luke 6:27-37**.
   'Love of enemies'
   Use the words of Jesus to design a 'Membership Card' for those who want to be his close followers.

   You may also add other things Jesus says about being a disciple, for example, **Mat 18:22**.

3. **(a)** Think of what would happen if everybody in school decided to:

   - continually forgive those who do wrong;

   - pray for those who treat them badly;

   - treat others as they would like to be treated themselves.

   (b) Choose two of the above and describe the effect it would have on the -

   - pupils,

   - teachers.

   You can present your answer as a role-play or written account.

Word Box

Mass   Holy Communion

Baptism   grace

St. Josephine Bakhita

Know the story of a person who showed great love for others

St. Josephine Bakhita is the first person from Sudan to be canonized. That means she is officially recognised by the Church as a saint. Before she died in 1947 she wrote to all young people.

Dear Children,

I'm here to tell you my life story, one that is probably very different from yours…

First of all, I want to tell you that God is a good Father and takes care of all his children: rich and poor; from every race and nation, no matter what colour or language.

Then… I want to let you know that God is good and he is always close to us, everywhere, even when we forget about him. He's close to those who are having a good time, those who are in tears, and those who suffer…

He knows that sometimes we don't treat each other like brothers and sisters should, and that's why the world around us is not as lovely as it could be. And so, children, I'm going to tell you my story, today, so that you can learn how to be more generous, be able to discover the beauty and goodness that is all around you, in the people you meet, in your friends and in everything that surrounds you. Then together, you will all be able to build a better world for those you will tell your story to…

My best wishes and all my love,
Yours, Bakhita

St. Josephine Bakhita

When Bakhita was just a girl in Sudan, Africa, her village was attacked and she was kidnapped, along with some women and children.

She describes what happened: "They took hold of me, threatened to harm me, and carried me off. Then we kept on walking for ages until we reached their village… and I don't know how long they kept me locked up there… I was alone, in the dark, crying for my mummy… One day they took me outside and I was sold to a trader with other children. Exhausted, we plodded on through the desert, walking on the sun-scorched sand. During the day it was hot and sticky; during the night it was sharp and cold."

Some days later they were taken to a slave market and sold like animals. A rich Arab chief bought Bakhita. At first, his family was kind to her. However, one day she accidentally dropped a precious vase. The master was furious, he took a whip and beat her so badly that it took ages for the wounds to heal.

Bakhita was then sold to a Turkish general. She describes what happened: "One day, my mistress decided that it was my turn, like all the other slaves to undergo the cruel process of tattooing. This consisted of making hundreds of cuts with a razor on my chest, stomach and arms. But when this was done they poured salt into the wounds so that the scars, instead of healing up, became inflamed and stayed visible forever… The pain was indescribable. I can truly say that the only reason I didn't die was that the Lord had better things in store for me."

When she was still a teenager in 1883, Bakhita was sold to an Italian family. They were kind and treated her well. When they returned to Italy, she came with them, and was given the job of looking after a young child called Mimmina. Eventually, Mimmina was sent to boarding school in Venice, and Bakhita went with her.

That was where she met the Daughters of Charity who ran the school, and where she started to learn about God, his Son Jesus, and Mary, the Mother of Jesus.

Soon, she received the Sacrament of Baptism and began to learn about the teaching of Jesus. She understood that she had to forgive the people who treated her badly and to pray for them.

One day, Bakhita decided she wanted to devote her entire life to Jesus whom she called 'The Master'. She joined the Daughters of Charity in December 1893.

For the next fifty years, Sister Bakhita worked tirelessly for the poor and for the Church. She was always happy, kind and humble.

She was a true witness to the goodness and love of God. When she grew old and weak, she was confined to a wheelchair. She spent her entire days praying for others and finding little ways to help them.

Bakhita died on 8 February 1947. On 1st October 2000, Pope John Paul II proclaimed her a saint – the first person from her country to be honoured by the Church in this way.

Activities

1. **(a)** Read Bakhita's letter and the story again.

   (b) What do you find surprising about the letter?

   (c) What do you think she would want you to remember about her life?

2. In what way do you think Bakhita's story could help you and others?

3. Imagine a book about saints is being written.

   What arguments would you use to persuade the author that Bakhita's story really needs to be included?

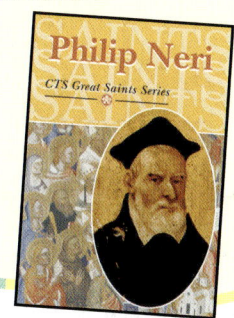

4. Find out what a SAINT is and write an explanation in your own words.

   Try: www.ainglkiss.com/saints/

5. Saint Nicholas was a person who showed great love to others.

   Find out about him and write a story of his life for Year 1 pupils with illustrations.

   Emphasise the parts of the story that are really important for the pupils.

   Or Choose another saint.

   Try: www.cptryon.org/prayer/child/nick.html

Word Box

canonize   saint

To Be A Disciple

Know how Jesus described a true disciple

Here is how Jesus describes a disciple, that is, a person who truly wants to be one of his faithful followers.

"I give you a new commandment:
love one another;
just as I have loved you,
you also must love one another.
By this love you have for one another,
everyone will know you are my disciples."
(John 13:34)

St. Paul explains what Jesus meant by love:
"Love is always patient and kind; it is never jealous; love is never boastful or conceited; it is never rude or selfish; it does not take offence, and is not resentful. Love takes no pleasure in other people's sins but delights in the truth; it is always ready to excuse, to trust, to hope, and to endure whatever comes."
(1 Cor 13:4-7)

St. John tells us:
"My children, our love is not to be just words or mere talk, but something real and active..."
(1 John 3:18)

Story of the true disciple

One day, Jesus told a parable to describe a true disciple. A parable is an earthly story with a heavenly meaning.

> "Everyone who comes to me and listens to my words and acts on them - I will show you what he is like.
>
> He is like the man who when he built his house dug, and dug deep, and laid the foundations on rock; when the river was in flood it bore down on that house, but could not shake it, it was so well built.
>
> But the one who listens and does nothing is like the man who built his house on soil, with no foundations: as soon as the river bore down on it, it collapsed; and what a ruin that house became!" (Luke 6:46-49)

Jesus is telling us that if we really want to follow him, we must listen to his words and put them into practice, not just make a promise and then forget about it.

Activities

1. Work in groups. Create a set of posters that will illustrate what St. Paul meant by love.
   For example: **love is kind.**

2. Work in groups. Study what St. Paul teaches us about love.

   (a) Write out a set of rules for how pupils should behave in class.

   (b) Then make a set of rules for what pupils should not do.

3. Think about yourself as a DISCIPLE of Jesus.

   (a) Copy the chart below and list all your thoughts on being a disciple.

   (b) Share what you write with the person beside you and explain your ideas to each other.

What is best about being a disciple	What might be difficult about being a disciple

Fr Damien

> Reflect on the life of a person who showed great love for those rejected by society

Here is a story of Damien, the leper, who listened to Jesus and acted on his words. He was born in 1840 in Belgium, in a family of eight children. He loved sport, especially speed skating.

He wanted to be a priest. At first, no one thought he was clever enough. He was sent as a missionary priest to Hawaii. Fr Damien was full of energy. He preached, baptised and heard confessions. He even built churches with his own hands.

Later on he heard of an island called Molokai. People suffering from an illness called leprosy were just left there with a few clothes, little food, and no houses.

People with leprosy get huge sores on their bodies, especially their hands and feet. Everyone knew you could catch it easily so they wanted to keep the sufferers away from everyone.

Damien went to go and look after them. He knew he would probably catch the disease, but he wanted to be like Jesus who had a special love for lepers.

At first he didn't find it easy, but he stayed and kept looking after the people and encouraging them to help each other. He nursed them, built a hospital and houses for them. He even dug graves for them when they died.

He built a church, and kept making it bigger, as more people kept coming. Then he started a choir, an orchestra and clubs. He wanted people to know how much Jesus loved them, especially when they were suffering.

Eventually, he did catch leprosy, died and was buried on the island. He was only 45 years old.

Activities

1. Fr Damien was a true disciple. Give examples from his life when he:

    (a) was compassionate;

    (b) thought about the needs of others before his own;

    (c) loved his neighbour as himself;

    (d) treated others as he would like to be treated himself.

2. Imagine what happened when Damien died and he met Jesus.

    Jesus wanted to thank him for all he had done and most especially for putting the Gospel into practice.

    Work in pairs to write out the conversation between Jesus and Damien.

3. Imagine you have been invited to make an appeal in your church one Sunday to raise money for a Leper Hospital.

    Write out your talk. Remember you want people to pray for the lepers and to give money to help them.

Project

4. Write a story, with illustrations, about somebody you know or have heard about, who is an inspirational person because he or she is a true follower of Jesus.

    Remember to give their name and nationality. You can write about:

    - What the person did or does.

    - Why you admire this person.

    - Why others should know about this person.

    - Where people will get more information.

5. Write a letter to the most inspirational person you know.
    - Say why you admire him or her.
    - Explain why you think this person's example is likely to help others.
    - Express your gratitude.

Word Box

preach   missionary

conceited   endure

4. Reconciliation

Please Sir!!

Reflect on wrong choices

PLEASE SIR!!
There's a fight - Sir!!
In the cloakrooms ... Sir!!
And Arnie's strangled Paul.
Smithy's strangled Watson
'Cos Watson took his ball.

Barney's ripped his shirt ... Sir,
And Baker sput on Sue.
She was only tryin' to stop them
And she's got it on her shoe ...
The helper lady went ... Sir,
She said she couldn't stay.
Jane's crying in the toilets
And the gerbil's got away ...

Garnett knocked the cage ... Sir,
The door, it just flipped back,
And it ran behind the cupboard
And it's stuck inside a crack.
We poked it with a stick ... Sir,
But the powder paint got spilt.
It's over all the carpet
And it's over Helen's kilt.
I think you ought to come ... Sir,
Mildred Miles was sick
And all the boys are yellin'
And Martin threw a brick.
It nearly hit John Baily.
And he's goin' to tell his mum,
So shall I say you're comin'
And shall I fetch his mum?
Shall we get the cleaners?
And I can mop the paint?

The new boy's torn his jacket
And he thinks he's going to faint ...
The other teacher said ... Sir,
That I should come to you
'Cos you're the Duty Teacher
So you'll know what to do Sir.

(Peter Dixon - 100 Best Poems for Children)

48

Activities

1. Imagine you are the Duty Teacher and you have got to sort out all that is happening.

    (a) What is the first thing you would do?

    (b) Do you think Arnie actually strangled Paul?
    How do you know?

    (c) What do Smithy and Watson need to do?

    (d) What would you say to Sue?

2. Work in groups.

    (a) Each person describes a time when someone got into trouble.

    (b) Explain how those actions affected others.

    (c) Explain how things were put right again.

    (d) Create a short role-play to illustrate one of the situations.

3. **(a)** Describe three things that usually upset people.

    (b) What advice would you give to someone your own age who is always getting into trouble?

My Actions Affect Others

Reflect on the consequences of our actions

We live in a world where we all depend on one another.

No one is an island!

No matter where we are or where we go, we will need to trust the people around us and they will want to trust us.

- What would happen at home if I was not willing to help?
- If I was always thinking only about myself, would I have friends?
- What happens in class if someone keeps messing about?
- How does the teacher feel when we misbehave?
- How does it feel when you are struggling to do your homework and someone helps you?
- What would happen if I cheat when I play sport?
- What would happen to the music group if some members did not practice.

How does it feel when someone praises you?

What's it like to be served a delicious meal when you're starving?

When we think about this jigsaw, we will see that what we do makes a difference to other people, and what other people do makes a difference to us. Sometimes we forget how our actions will affect others.

We need to reflect on how we may cause unhappiness, and the way we are capable of bringing joy to other people as well.

Activities

1. **(a)** Draw a picture of yourself on an island.

   (b) Draw arrows going onto the island - and list all the things you depend on from others for today.

   (c) Now draw arrows coming out of the island - list all the things others rely on you for today.

2. What do you think is the meaning of the words '**No one is an island**'?

3. **(a)** Choose two of the pieces of the jigsaw and copy them into your book.

   (b) Think through the different consequences of the actions in each situation.

   (c) Design your own jigsaw pieces to fit them and write in the consequences of the actions. For help, look at the example in the box below.

Example - If I was not willing to help at home:

- My Mum would have a lot of work to do.
- Everybody would nag at me.
- I would know I was being selfish.

What is Sin?

> Know that sin hurts us, others and our relationship with God

Each night before going to bed we should spend some time thanking Jesus for all the good things that have come to us during the day.

Then we need to think about the things that have gone badly - maybe somebody has said or done something that hurt us or maybe we feel bad about what we said or did. If it is something serious that we did, we ask Jesus to help us put it right.

When we deliberately choose to do what we know is wrong, it is a sin. We know, for certain, that God will always forgive us if we are sorry for our sins. We can say 'sorry' to God at any time. When something bad happens that is beyond our control, it is not a sin.

What is sin?

- A failure to love God and others.
- Choosing to do something hurtful rather than good.
- Deliberately doing what we know to be wrong.

Are all sins serious?

Yes, but some are more than others. For a sin to be very serious -

- it has to be something very wrong;
- you know that it is very wrong;
- you freely choose to do it.

Venial sins

Venial sins are less serious, but we have to make an effort to avoid committing them, or they could lead to a more serious sin.

What does it mean to be truly sorry for our sins?

First, *we have to know and understand -*

- what we have done wrong;

- how we have hurt the other person;

- that sin separates us from God.

Second, *we must -*
- want to receive forgiveness from God;

- be prepared to say 'sorry' to the person we hurt;

- be prepared to put things right where we can;

- be prepared to try hard not to offend again.

Third, *remember -*

- God is love.

- He will always love us.

God is Love and anyone who lives in love lives in God, and God Lives in him

(1 Jn 4:16)

Think about the following situations...

"They dared us to put a huge lump of concrete onto the railway line. We knew it could derail a train and people could be killed. But we were fast runners and we knew we would get away with it. Unfortunately, the police caught us and before we knew it we were in their van." **(The Gang)**

"We were having a contest to see which of us could throw stones the furthest and actually hit a passing train – we knew it was wrong to do it, but it was great fun." **(Lisa and her friends)**

"One day I sneaked out of school to go to the park with my friend. When I got home I pretended I had been to school. My parents believed me. I felt bad about it so I told them I had been lying because I felt so guilty. They were glad I had owned up but disappointed I had let them down." **(Oliver)**

"I felt terrible when I broke my mum's favourite vase. We were playing around in the living room and it fell on the floor. She cried and I felt awful, especially as I had bought it for her. I told her I was really sorry and I bought her some flowers. I think she forgave me." **(Jessica)**

Activities

Jessica, Oliver, Lisa and her friends and the Gang all did something wrong.

1. **(a)** Which of the actions was the most serious?

   (b) Was it a sin?

   (c) Which action was not a sin?

2. **(a)** What was the main difference between what Lisa and her friends and the Gang were doing?

   (b) If you had been with Lisa and her friends what would you have done?

3. One boy in the Gang was very upset because he was caught.

   Another boy was very upset because he realised he was putting people's lives at risk.

   (a) Which of the two boys was upset for the right reasons?

   (b) Imagine you are the police officer. How would you explain to the boys what was wrong about their actions?

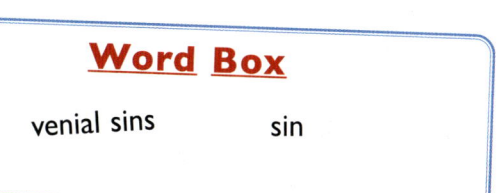

Word Box

venial sins   sin

A Story of God's Love and Forgiveness

Know and understand the story of the lost son

The Parable of the Lost Son

Jesus used the story of a young man to show us how God is always ready to forgive those who repent and turn back to him.

One day, a young son asked his father for all the money he was likely to get when his father died and off he went to enjoy himself. He cared more for himself than for his family.

Before long, the son became lonely, frightened and afraid because of what he had done. He had run out of money and found a job feeding pigs. He was even tempted to eat the pig food because he was so hungry. His selfishness and greed caused him a great deal of pain and unhappiness. All the time he was away, his father was suffering too. He missed his son. He worried about where he was and what he was doing, and he longed to have him home again, where he could tell him how much he loved him.

His older brother also suffered because he watched his father's sadness. He probably felt angry that his brother had caused so much upset. Also, he felt angry that he was being faithful and loyal to his father, but his efforts were not recognised, because his father was too busy worrying over his younger son. He was jealous.

Eventually, when the son returned home the father welcomed him with open arms and put on a great party to celebrate. But the older son stayed away. He could not let go of his jealousy and therefore was unable to celebrate with his brother. (Lk 15:11-32)

What can we learn from this parable?

The younger son shows us — how our selfishness (or sin) hurts ourselves, other people, and our relationship with God.

The father shows us — how God loves us regardless of what we do.

It is we who turn away from God.

The older son shows us — that we can be jealous even though most of the time we do the right thing.

Jealousy weakens our relationship with God and others.

Activities

1. What do you think is the most important message that Jesus wants us to learn from the parable of the Lost Son?

2. Imagine your school has invited an artist to paint a picture of this parable. What instructions would you want to give to the artist, so that he would highlight the important parts of the story?

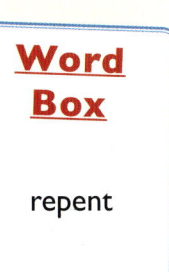

Word Box

repent

Forgiveness is not Easy

Understand that God loves us and forgives us if we are truly sorry

We know that there are times when it is very difficult to ask for forgiveness.

Before we ask for forgiveness, we have to look closely at the damage we have done.

This is painful because it means we have to change our behaviour.

It also means we have to admit that we were in the wrong and that's not easy.

It is certainly not easy to forgive when we have really been hurt.

There are times when we feel more like taking revenge, or 'getting even' with the person who hurt us.

On such occasions, it helps to know that there is a difference between **making a decision to forgive** and not to take revenge and **feeling like forgiving**.

We can't always feel like forgiving, but with God's help we can make a decision to forgive.

Jesus asks us to forgive Not 7 But 77!

One day Peter asked Jesus should he forgive up to seven times. To his surprise, Jesus replied, "Not seven, I tell you, but seventy-seven times."

When asked about forgiving enemies, Jesus asks us not only to forgive our enemies but to:

'do good to those who hate you and pray for those who persecute you'.

On another occasion, Jesus explained to his disciples that if somebody has something against them, before going to worship God, they should make peace with that person. (Matt 5:23-24)

Jesus shows us how to forgive

When Jesus was being crucified on the Cross he asked his heavenly Father to forgive those who were crucifying him because they did not know what they were doing.

He even made excuses for those driving the nails into him. Jesus refused to take revenge or to 'get even' even though it costs him everything.

Forgiveness is a gift

Forgiveness is a gift from God. It is not something we can achieve ourselves - we have to ask Jesus to help us to forgive. He has promised us:

*"If you remain in me
and my words remain in you,
you may ask what you will
and you shall get it."* (John 15:7)

Activities

1. Put the following statements in order of difficulty for you. Give a reason why the one at the top of your list is very difficult.

   The most difficult thing about saying sorry is:

   (a) actually saying 'sorry' and really meaning it;

   (b) seeing the hurt you have caused someone else;

   (c) wondering what others may think of you;

   (d) not knowing how to show you are sorry;

   (e) having to face the consequences of your actions.

2. Think about why we find it difficult to say sorry.

   Write a short prayer to ask God to give you the faith and courage to say sorry, no matter how difficult you may find it.

Word Box

revenge   forgiveness

Sacrament of Reconciliation

> Understand the importance of the Sacrament of Reconciliation

Jesus gave the Apostles power to forgive sins when he said:

"As the Father sent me, so I am sending you."

After saying this he breathed on them and said:

"Receive the Holy Spirit. For those whose sins you forgive, they are forgiven…" (John 20:21)

Through the Apostles, this power has been handed on to the bishops and priests. They continue to pass on to us God's love and mercy through the Sacrament of Reconciliation. Sometimes we call this Confession.

Every time we receive the Sacrament of Reconciliation it marks a new beginning in our lives. It is a chance for us to leave behind all the wrongs we have done and to start again.

Before receiving the Sacrament of Reconciliation we spend some time thinking seriously about what we have done.

We think of the times when we have failed to love. It might have been when we:

- told a lie;
- said something hurtful;
- were selfish;
- took something that belonged to another person.

This is a time when we have to be honest with ourselves and not make excuses for what we have done.

We have to listen to the inner voice inside us, which we call our **conscience**, to tell us what we have done wrong.

In Confession, the priest is there to help us.

He represents God and through him we receive God's forgiveness.

We know for certain that the priest will **never** repeat anything told in confession.

Examining our conscience

Examining my conscience...
I think about how I have behaved...

- at home...
- with others
- at school...
- ...with friends
- ...towards God
- by myself...

I listen to my inner voice...

The main parts of the Sacrament of Reconciliation

Confession
I ask the priest for a blessing and tell him my sins.

Penance
The priest either asks me to say a prayer or do something to try to put things right.

Sorrow
The priest asks me to say the Act of Contrition.

Forgiveness
The priest says the words of absolution and I receive God's forgiveness for all my sins.

Activities

1. Your friend is not sure of the difference between something that happens by accident and something that is a sin.

   Here is one example of an accident. Imagine you were putting away some glasses for your mum and let one drop on the floor and it broke.

   (a) Can you give another example of an accident?

   (b) Now give an example of something that would be a sin.

Going to Confession

Know what happens during the Sacrament of Reconciliation

Before Confession

1. Think about what I have done to displease God and others.

2. Pray for grace to be truly sorry for my sins.

3. Tell God that I want to change and turn back to him.

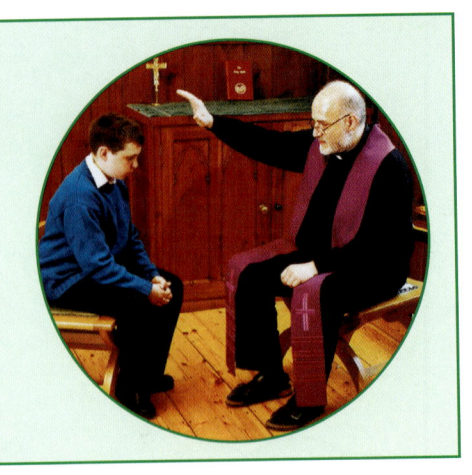

At Confession

1. I tell the priest how long it is since my last Confession.

2. I tell him the things I have done wrong on purpose.

3. The priest will give me a penance.

4. I tell God that I am really sorry - and say an Act of Contrition.

5. God forgives me through the words of the priest.

6. I say 'thank you' to the priest.

After Confession

1. I say my penance, or think about what the priest has asked me to do.

2. I thank God for his forgiveness and love.

> **An Act of Contrition (sorrow)**
>
> *Oh my God,*
> *because you are so good,*
> *I am very sorry that I have sinned against you,*
> *and by the help of your grace,*
> *I will not sin again.*

Activities

1. Copy the Act of Contrition into your own book. Learn it and underline the words that are important.

2. Design a card with instructions on how to receive the Sacrament of Reconciliation for children making their First Confession.

3. Imagine that a friend who is not a Catholic has asked you to explain what the Sacrament of Reconciliation is about. Write down what you would say.

4. What did Jesus say about forgiveness?

   Use these bible references to help you. **Luke 17:4, Matt 6:12, Matt 18:22**.

5. How should we behave after receiving this Sacrament?

6. Re-read the poem 'Please Sir!' on page 48.

   (a) In pairs, make a list of some of the difficult situations your teacher has to sort out.

   (b) Suggest ways in which you and your friends can help the teacher.

Word Box

| conscience | contrition | | absolution |
| penance | Reconciliation | Sacrament | displease | confession |

5. Life in the Risen Lord

A Gift from God

> Know and understand that Jesus is risen from the dead

Jesus is alive and we have seen him!

The most sensational news that the disciples ever heard was that Jesus had risen from the dead. They had seen him crucified on Good Friday. They could not understand why this should happen to their Lord and Master. Two whole days had passed and now they were astounded by the news that some women had brought to them. The women had gone to the tomb in the early morning and the body was no longer there. They had seen a vision of angels who declared he was alive.

The disciples reacted in different ways: some thought it was just pure nonsense. Peter went running to the tomb and then back home, amazed at what had happened. (John 24:12) Thomas would not believe anybody. He said: "Unless I see the holes that the nails made in his hands and can put my finger into the holes they made, and unless I can put my hand into his side I refuse to believe." (John 20:25) Here is an account of what Mary of Magdala did:

Mary woke early that Sunday morning. Her mind was full of the events of Friday.

Then she remembered she wanted to finish washing and anointing her Lord's body.

"Where was he?"

"Why had they done this"

"Who had taken him?"

Quickly, Mary set off up the hill. It was a crisp, bright morning.

As she made her way towards the tomb she thought about what had happened, and more importantly, what might happen now!

Finally, she reached the garden. At once she noticed the tomb was open. The stone had been rolled away.

She looked round but saw no one. Then she rushed into the tomb: the body was gone.

Her mind full of questions, Mary raced back down the hill to tell Peter and John. The disciples checked it out for themselves and went to tell the others.

Meantime, Mary stayed outside the tomb weeping. After a short while she stooped to have a look inside.

A radiant light filled the darkness and two angels sat where the body of Jesus had been.

"Why are you weeping?" asked the angels. Mary told them that her Lord had been taken and she didn't know where they had put him.

As she turned round a stranger was standing behind her and he said, "Woman, why are you weeping? Who are you looking for?"

Mary was very upset and she looked pleadingly at the stranger. "Sir, if you have taken him away, tell me where you have put him and I will go and get him."

"Mary." This one word, the sound of the voice. Could it be? Yes, it was!

"Rabbuni," cried Mary, hardly daring to believe that it was the Lord.

"Do not cling to me Mary, because I have not yet ascended to my Father."

Jesus then told Mary to go and tell the other disciples she had seen him.

Mary left to do as he asked, turning back continually to see her Master. Then she broke into a run, tearing through the streets, desperately trying to reach the house where the others were gathered. She burst through the door.

"I've seen the Lord," she cried. The disciples looked at her in amazement, and sat attentively as she told them everything Jesus had said and done. It had been an amazing day for everyone.
(John 20:1-18 adapted)

Activities

1. **(a)** Read the story of Mary of Magdala again.

   (b) Identify the important moments in it.

   (c) Think about a time when your own feelings changed from sorrow to joy.

2. Work in groups of four: write a play to dramatise the story of Mary of Magdala using the text above and the points below to help you.

   - Narrator: describes the scene.

   - Mary: what she says when she discovers that the tomb is empty.

   - Angels: what they say.

   - Jesus: what he says to Mary.

   - Mary: what she says to Jesus.

Word Box

tomb   Rabbuni

3. Class divides into five groups: choose two members of each group to be police officers.

Imagine news of the resurrection of Jesus has spread around Jerusalem, but the police cannot find him.

All those who claim to have seen him are rounded up by the police and are brought to court to be questioned. You are among them. **Each group will be questioned by two police officers.**

GROUP 1 - The disciples and Thomas (John 20:19-29)

GROUP 2 - The disciples on the Road to Emmaus (Luke 24:13-35)

GROUP 3 - The Apostles gathered together (Luke 24:36-43)

GROUP 4 - On the shore of Tiberias (John 21:1-14)

GROUP 5 - Peter with an eyewitness (John 21:15-17)

DISCIPLES
The teacher will give each group a copy of their story. They must study it carefully and agree on all the facts.

POLICE
The police can work together to plan the questions they want to ask.

PUBLIC
The public can phone-in to prompt the police to ask other questions. When you are not giving evidence you can be among the public.

JUDGE'S SUMMARY
The teacher will sum up the evidence and decide how complete it is.

Questions from the Police:

(a) What did you think had happened to the body?

(b) Did you go to the tomb or where did you see him?

(c) How do you know it was Jesus and not a ghost?

(d) How did your friends react when you told them you had seen Jesus?

(e) Did Jesus ever tell you he would rise from the dead, and did you believe him?

(f) What do you think is going to happen now?

Jesus is with us

Know that Jesus is present among us in different ways

Know that I am with you always; yes, to the end of time (Matt 28:20)

These were the last words that Jesus left with his disciples before he ascended into heaven.

Jesus is present in different ways in the world today. He is present in each person who believes in him and has received the Sacrament of Baptism. He inspires each one of us to use our skills and talents to do his work.

When we visit a church we know Jesus is present in a particular way in the Blessed Sacrament.

Jesus is present in all the sacraments. In the Mass, we receive Jesus in the Sacrament of the Eucharist. He is truly present in us when we receive him in Holy Communion.

In the Sacrament of Reconciliation, Jesus is present and wants to give us the grace and help we need to lead a good life.

When we read and reflect on the words of Jesus in the Gospels, he is present and speaks to us through them.

Jesus is also present when we pray. He listens and responds to all our prayers, answering them in the way which is best for us.

Jesus works through us

We believe Jesus is present in us through the Sacrament of Baptism and the other Sacraments. Because of this, he is able to work through us, particularly when we behave as he would. St. Francis is one example of someone who reflects the love, peace and forgiveness that Jesus wants us to show to others.

When we are kind to others, people can see something of Jesus in us. Here is the prayer St. Francis used to ask Jesus to work through him:

Lord, make me an instrument of your peace.
Where there is hatred, let me sow love;
where there is injury, pardon;
where there is doubt, faith;
where there is despair, hope;
where there is darkness, light;
where there is sadness, joy.

Activities

1. Work in pairs.

   Read the prayer of St. Francis again.

   Suggest ways to show how you could be an instrument of peace so that:

   (a) where there is injury, you could bring pardon;

   (b) where there is despair, you could bring hope;

   (c) where there is doubt, you could bring faith;

   (d) where there is sadness, you could bring joy.

2. We believe that Jesus is present in different ways.

   Read page 68 again. Choose one of the following, and use signs, symbols and words to explain how we can experience the presence of Jesus.

   - The Sacrament of Baptism.
   - The Sacrament of Reconciliation.
   - The Mass.
   - Prayer.

   ### Word Box
   Mass Apostles sacrament pardon disciples Eucharist Tiberias Holy Communion resurrection

Prayer is being with Jesus

Know that there are different ways of praying

There are many different ways of praying - the way that is likely to work best is the one you like most.

Prayer is about growing close to Jesus. It is about talking to him, telling him our troubles and joys. It also means listening to him. Jesus is our best companion and friend; he hears everything we say when we speak to him.

Sometimes we can find a quiet place to be alone with Jesus and talk to him about everything that is happening and ask him to help us. This is called vocal prayer.

We can take a story from a gospel, read it over very slowly and allow Jesus to speak to us in it. This prayer is called meditation.

We can also pray to Jesus in silence: looking at a picture or statue of him to help us. This prayer is called contemplation.

Guidance for praying

(a) Try to be still, be relaxed and be attentive.

(b) Have your own place and time for prayer. It does not matter where or when.

(c) Pray every day. Don't give up. Even if it seems difficult, keep trying. Jesus is with you.

(d) Pray in the way that suits you best.

Types of Prayer

Prayer of Petition or Asking:

When we ask Jesus for help for ourselves or for someone else.

Prayer of Sorrow:

When we say sorry to Jesus for something we have done wrong and ask for forgiveness.

Prayer of Thanksgiving:

When we thank Jesus.

Prayer of Praise:

When we sing a hymn of praise.

Prayer of Meditation:

When we read a passage from scripture and think about it.

Prayer of Contemplation:

When we pray to Jesus in silence.

When I want to pray

When I want to pray
I don't put on a face
Or search for a desert
Or other such place
I can pray at my ease
Any place I can find,
Whether sitting or kneeling,
The Lord doesn't mind.

(Christy Kenneally from 'Miracles and Me', Paulist Press, 1986.)

Activities

1. What type of prayer would we say if we wanted to:

    (a) ask Jesus to help somebody who was sick?

    (b) tell Jesus we are sorry for doing something wrong?

    (c) thank Jesus when something wonderful has happened?

    (d) stay close to Jesus to be with him?

2. Draw a clock face.

    Divide it into sections to show the time you spend asleep, eating, playing, at school, watching TV and praying.

    Or make a chart to list all the times each week when we pray in different ways.

    For example:

    - we pray at the start of the school day...

    - we pray with our families when.... .

---

vocal prayer   meditation   **Word Box**   contemplation   petition

Activities

3. **(a)** Read and think about the poem 'When I want to pray'.

   (b) Describe what you do when you want to pray.

4. You are invited to enter a competition.

   - Your task is to make a Prayer Book suitable for young people aged 6-10 years old.

     You will need to include well-known prayers, old and new, and some of your own.

   - You should use your ICT skills and put your prayer book on a disk which you can send to the CTS, the publisher of this book.

     The three best entries that arrive before the end of July each year, will be put on the website - *www.tere.org*.

   - Start by writing an introduction to your Prayer Book on how people can pray.

Research

5. Research the web site *http://www.cptryon.org/prayer/child/index.html*

   On this site you should find Prayers of the Church, Everyday Prayers and Prayers for Special Seasons.

   You can select some of these to put into your Prayer Book.

Importance of Prayer

Reflect on Jesus' teaching and example on prayer

We all like to spend time chatting to our friends, telling them our news, sharing our problems and having a good laugh about things we have done. We get to know Jesus by spending time talking and listening to him.

Jesus spent a lot of time in prayer. Frequently, he found a quiet place to be alone to pray.

Jesus has given us clear instructions about praying

"And when you pray, do not imitate the hypocrites: they love to say their prayers standing up in the synagogues and at the street corners for people to see them. I tell you solemnly, they have had their reward.

But when you pray, go to your private room and, when you have shut the door, pray to your Father who is in that secret place, and your Father who sees all that is done in secret will reward you." (Matt 6:5-6)

How we should pray

"In your prayers do not babble as the pagans do, for they think that by using many words they will make themselves heard. Do not be like them; your Father knows what you need before you ask him:

'Our Father in heaven,
may your name be held holy,
your kingdom come,
your will be done,
on earth as in heaven...' (Matt 6:7-10)

The Pharisee and the Tax Collector

Here is a parable or story that Jesus told his followers in order to explain to them how they should pray.

Narrator - Jesus reminds us that it is important to be humble when we pray.

Jesus - A Pharisee and a tax collector went to the Temple to pray. The Pharisee stood in the Temple, where everyone could see him and prayed in a very loud voice.

Pharisee - I thank God that I am not like that tax collector over there. I am not greedy or dishonest like other people. I am a good man. I give money to the poor and fast during the week.

Jesus - The Pharisee obviously wanted everyone to know he was good.

However, the tax collector stayed very quietly at the back of the Temple, not even daring to look up to God. He said,

Tax Collector - God, have mercy on me a sinner.

Jesus - I tell you that the tax collector was the one who pleased God most of all because his prayers were humble. Everyone who makes himself great will be humbled, and everyone who humbles himself will be made great. (Luke 18:9-14)

Activities

1. **(a)** Discuss with the person next to you what you think is the most important part of the story of the Pharisee and tax collector?

   (b) Write what you think is the main difference between the prayer of the Pharisee and the prayer of the tax collector.

2. Imagine you are Jesus and write a letter to the Pharisee to help him understand how he should pray.

3. Re-write the story of the Pharisee and the tax collector with modern characters and draw the scene.

   For example, a football hooligan could be one of them.

4. Find a Morning and Night Prayer to put into your prayer book.

Word Box

hypocrite   Temple

fast   synagogue   pagans

The Our Father

> Know and understand the Our Father

When the Apostles asked Jesus to teach them to pray he taught them the Our Father. (Luke 11:1-4)

It is a prayer of praise and petition to God. The prayer is split into seven parts. The first three parts give glory to God and the last four ask God for help.

Notice the opening words of the prayer: *"Our Father"*.

These words remind us that we are children of God; he is our loving Father and we can talk to him about anything.

The Parts of the Our Father

Our Father, who art in heaven, hallowed be thy name:
This tells us that God is a loving Father and we should remember to keep God's name holy.

Thy kingdom come:
This means we should be building God's kingdom of love and kindness towards all people on earth, now.

Thy will be done on earth as it is in heaven:
This reminds us that we must try to do God's will each and every day of our lives.

Give us this day our daily bread:
This is a request that God will provide everything we need.

Forgive us our trespasses as we forgive those who trespass against us:
In this we are asking God to forgive us when we do something wrong. But we must also forgive those who have done something wrong to us.

And lead us not into temptation:
Here we ask God not to let us take the path that leads to sin.

Deliver us from evil:
We ask God to watch over us and protect us from harm and evil.

Activities

1. Copy out the Our Father. Colour the phrases as follows;
   Those that:-

   - ask God for things - **BLUE**

   - talk about the way God wants us to live - **GREEN**

   - talk about the power of God - **RED**

   - talk about forgiveness - **YELLOW**

   Word Box
   hallowed   trespasses
   Kingdom of God
   deliver   temptation

2. Answer the following questions in your book.

   (a) How do we make sure that God's name is kept holy and respected?

   (b) List three things you would ask for in prayer; remember God supplies our needs not our wants!

3. Work in pairs to create a role-play to demonstrate being tempted and how to resist the temptation.

4. Work in groups to pray the 'Our Father' at an assembly.

   (a) Select some background music to go with the words.

   (b) Now put actions that will express the meanings of the words.

5. Write down what you think are the two most important things in the prayer 'Our Father'.
   For an explanation of the Our Father try:

   http://www.cptryon.org/prayer/child/father.html

The Rosary

Learn how to pray the Rosary

The Rosary is a prayer honouring Our Lady. It is split into four groups called:- **The Joyful Mysteries, The Mysteries of Light, The Sorrowful Mysteries and The Glorious Mysteries.**

Special beads, known as 'Rosary beads' are used to say the Rosary. These beads help a person to pray a certain number of 'Hail Marys'.

So instead of thinking about the number of times we say the 'Hail Mary' we think about certain times in the life of Jesus and Mary - these are called the 'mysteries'.

Each set of mysteries has five "decades" in it. A decade means a group of ten prayers.

A decade starts with one 'Our Father', then ten 'Hail Marys' and ends with a 'Glory Be to the Father'.

As we pray each decade we think about a different event in the life of Jesus or Mary. As our fingers touch the beads and our voices say the words, our minds imagine the scene and we open our hearts to Jesus.

The Glorious Mysteries

First mystery: The Resurrection of Jesus from the dead.

Second: The Ascension of Jesus into Heaven.

Third: The Descent of the Holy Spirit on the Apostles.

Fourth: The Assumption of Our Lady into Heaven, - when Mary was taken into heaven, body and soul, because she had never broken her relationship with God.

Fifth: The Crowning of Mary as Queen of Heaven. Mary is the Queen of all the Saints because she is the most perfect of all God's creation.

Activities

1. Read the section again on the Glorious Mysteries.

   The Fourth & Fifth Mysteries have an explanation with them.

   Write a similar explanation for the first three mysteries.

2. Work in groups of five.

   Each person should draw one of the five Glorious Mysteries.

   Then put them together as a mosaic or booklet with a short explanation of each one.

3. Design a card: the title 'The Rosary'.

   Give an explanation of how to say the rosary and how it helps us to pray.

Research

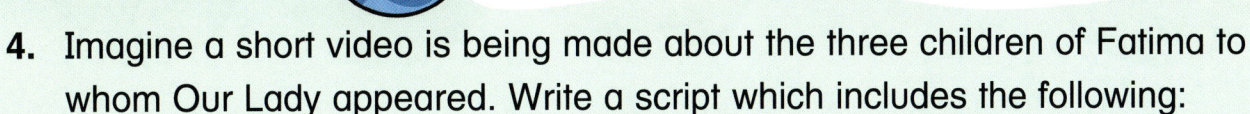

4. Imagine a short video is being made about the three children of Fatima to whom Our Lady appeared. Write a script which includes the following:

   - Where is Fatima?

   - Why did Our Lady ask the children to say the rosary?

   - What did Our Lady promise the children?

Try: http://cmri.org/message.htm
The Fatima Message

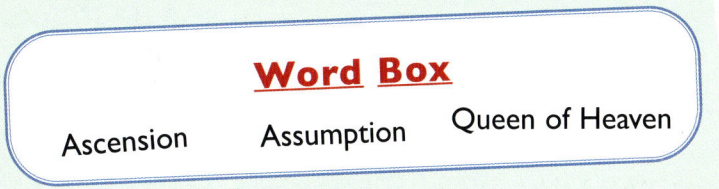

Word Box

Ascension   Assumption   Queen of Heaven

6. People of other Faiths

World Faiths

Reflect on different beliefs in our country

There are many religions and beliefs as well as Christianity in this country.

Different religions have some things in common.

Most religions have:

- a set of beliefs;
- a set of rules to guide behaviour;
- a way of worshipping.

Snapshot of some World Faiths

Here is a snapshot of some world faiths. Remember this is just to give you an idea of each faith. There is far more to say than we have space for here.

Religions

Judaism began with **Abraham.** The followers of Judaism are called **Jews**.

Hinduism has no single founder. Its followers are called **Hindus.**

Buddhism began with an Indian prince **Siddartha Gautama.** Its followers are called **Buddhists.**

Islam was made known to people by the Prophet **Muhammad.** The followers of Islam are called **Muslims.**

Guru Nanak started the **Sikh** religion. Its followers are called **Sikhs.**

Beliefs

Jews believe in one God who is caring, ever present and invisible.

Most **Hindus** believe in one god, Brahman. The gods of the Hindu faith represent different expressions of Brahman.

Buddhists do not believe in God.

Muslims believe there is only one God called Allah who is all-knowing and all-powerful.

Sikhs believe there is only one God who is Creator and has no form.

Behaviour

Jews try to lead good lives and believe in justice. Family life is very important for them.

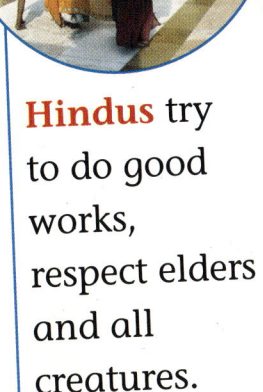

Hindus try to do good works, respect elders and all creatures.

Buddhists try to be gentle towards all things, live in peace and not be selfish.

Muslims try to be honest, modest and respectful

Sikhs try to avoid anger, greed and pride. Kindness and humility are very important.

Worship

Jews pray several times a day. They worship in a **synagogue.** Their holy book is called the **Torah.**

Hindus offer prayers and small gifts of fruit and other things to their gods. This act of worship is called **Puja.** They worship in the home and in the **temple.**

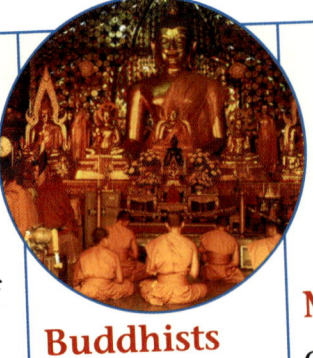

Buddhists meditate using candles, flowers and incense and a statue of the Buddha to help them. They worship at home and in a **temple.**

Muslims are called to prayer five times daily. Their holy book is called the **Qur'an.** Their place of worship is called a **mosque.**

Sikhs meditate using their holy book **Guru Granth Sahib.** Their place of worship is called **Gurdwara.**

Activities

1. There were many words that might be new to you in the information about world faiths. Here is a box containing some of these words.

   | Hindu | Gurdwara | Muslim | Torah | Puja | Buddha | Muhammad |
   | Qur'an | | Synagogue | | Guru Granth Sahib | Mosque | Sikh |

   (a) Pick out from the box one word for each world faith (four words altogether).

   (b) Explain what each word means.

Activities

2. Imagine you have received the following email from Nathan, a Jewish boy, you met on holiday and he wants to get to know you.

Write a reply to Nathan.

To...
cc...
Subject:

Hi,
It was good to meet you last week. I am a Jew and I would like to know what your religion is.

Can you tell me something about it, for example, what is your most important holy day and what you do on it?

This is what I do: every Saturday with my family I observe the Sabbath and keep its laws and customs.

We have a special meal together. Candles are lit and there are Sabbath blessings, prayers, songs and readings.

We don't go shopping or watch TV on that day!
Nathan

Word Box

belief   worship   customs   Sabbath

Other Religions

Reflect on other religions

Have you ever wondered how many other religions there are?
The table below shows some different religions and an estimate of how many believers there are in that religion.

RELIGION	Numbers of believers (approximately)	Began when? (approximately)
Judaism	14 million	1800-1400 BC
Hinduism	900 million	1500 BC
Buddhism	360 million	523 BC
Christianity	2000 million	28 AD
Islam	1300 million	622 AD
Sikhism	23 million	1500 AD

Activities

1. What surprised you about these figures and what was it that you expected?

2. Why do you think we can't say for sure how many people belong to each religion?

3. Which religion in the list is the oldest religion?

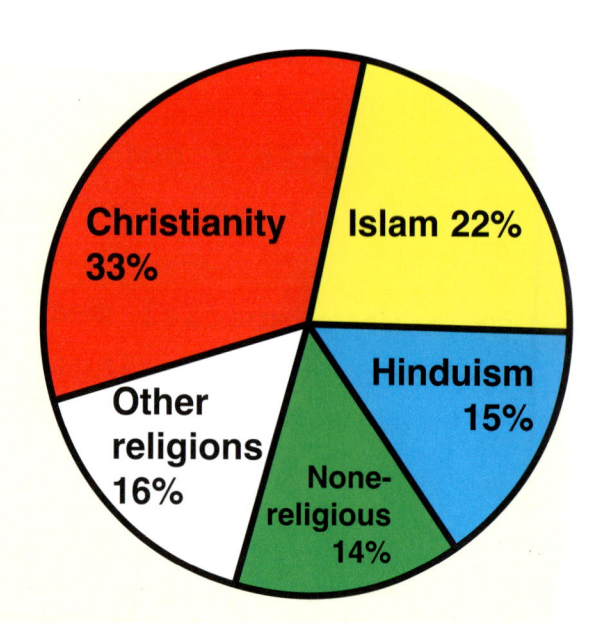

4. Which religion in the list is the youngest religion?

5. Which religion has the most people who belong to it?

Christianity 33%
Islam 22%
Hinduism 15%
None-religious 14%
Other religions 16%

84

Religion is not just about numbers, it is about what people believe. Read the bubbles below:

> I wear a wrist band (kara) which reminds me of my belief in God. When I see the band I remember that I must not do anything that would offend against my **Sikh** religion.

> Before starting work, I have a bath and offer worship to images of **Hindu** gods. I place some flowers in front of the images and light a joss stick. Then I read a short prayer.

> Almost everything I do reminds me of my Jewish faith, even the food we eat.

Activities

6. **(a)** Design your own bubble and in it write words that reflect what you do as a Christian.

    (b) Design something that you could wear to remind you that you are a Christian. e.g. a badge.

7. Work in Groups. Discuss the things around the school building which tell people this is a Christian school.

Christianity and other Religions

> Reflect on similarities and differences between Christianity and other religions

Different beliefs

You may think all religions look quite similar because they have so many things in common, but there are also many different beliefs.

Beliefs about behaviour

If you asked a Hindu, Muslim, Christian, Jew and Sikh to write down some examples of good behaviour and of bad behaviour, they would probably agree on a lot of things. People of many different faiths would agree with most of the Ten Commandments.

Beliefs about the Universe

There are more differences here. Jews, Christians and Muslims believe that God created everything from nothing and that the universe has a beginning and end.

But Hindus believe that the universe goes through cycles of birth, death and rebirth.

Beliefs about the human being

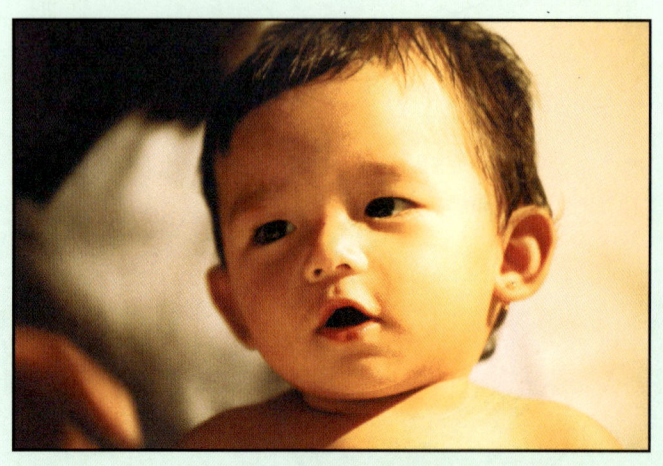

Are you - body and soul - unique, a one off? Yes, say Jews, Christians and Muslims. There will never be another you.

Hindus and Sikhs believe in **reincarnation**.

This means that they believe the 'real you' lives in the 'shell' of a body. At death, your soul passes on to another body, perhaps as a human, perhaps not. This cycle of birth, death and rebirth Hindus call **Samsara**.

Places of worship

Go round a synagogue, a Jewish place of worship, and you will not find any holy pictures or statues.

A Synagogue, a Jewish place of worship.

A mosque or a Muslim place of worship does not have statues or images of holy people.

A Mosque, an Islamic place of worship.

Jews and Muslims believe that using images in worship is wrong, since they say God cannot be represented by images.

Go round a Hindu temple and you will often find plenty of pictures and statues.

Outside a Hindu temple, a Hindu place of worship.

The majority of Hindu homes have a shrine. A shrine can be anything from a room, or a small altar or simply pictures or statues of gods expressed in many forms.

Christians often use holy pictures, statues and objects to help them pray. They do not worship the pictures and statues themselves.

The Holy Spirit. Stained glass window, St Peter's Rome.

Many churches have stained glass windows. Sometimes, they represent events from the Bible or the lives of saints.

Activities

1. **(a)** Read below what believers of various faiths say about their faith.

   (b) To which religion does each person belong?

Shenila,
I believe there is only one God. Allah. There should be no statues or pictures to try to show God. This is idol-worship. There is also no such thing as reincarnation. When people die they are judged by God. They do not come back to earth again.

Armitraj,
I believe in one God. Any religion that says there is more than one god is false. I also believe in reincarnation. When I die, my soul may enter a new body and be born again.

David,
Every day I say a prayer that begins. 'Listen; O Israel, the Lord is One...' I believe totally that there is only one God. I believe that God chose my ancestors, to be a holy people. I don't believe in reincarnation.

Barvana,
In my faith, I pray to many gods. Vishnu is my favourite. I believe he protects me. I also believe in reincarnation.

Activities

2. What do Jews and Muslims believe about God that is also true for Christians?

3. Would you say the four believers on page 88 have any beliefs in common? Explain.

4. What might you see in a Hindu temple that you would not see in a Mosque?

Research

5. You can find out about a particular religion's beliefs by some of the practices you find in that religion. Here are a few.

Pick one, and try to find out a few reasons why they have this practice.

    (a) Muslims may carry a prayer mat (and a compass) with them on their way to work. Why?

    (b) Sikh men wear turbans and have beards. Why?

(c) Most Hindus are vegetarians. Why?

Word Box

idols   turban

How should Christians relate to believers of other Faiths

> Know what the Catholic Church teaches about our relations with other faiths

As Christians, we believe we can learn from other faiths. However, we believe that Jesus was the unique revelation of God. That means that Jesus came to show us what God was like. He is both true God and true man.

The Catholic Church teaches us that we must not reject anything that is true and holy in other religions.

We must love other people as ourselves. The fact that they belong to other religions must not prevent us from loving them.

Jesus is the Way, the Truth and the Life. He has come to save us and it is through him that we will have eternal life with God. We should hold fast to what we believe to be true.

As followers of Jesus, we are called to show love and compassion to others by our actions and lives.

Letters to Sr Magdeleine

Dear Sr Magdeleine,
How should I treat other people who do not believe in Jesus?

Dear Sr Magdeleine,
My friend says it does not matter which religion you believe in. Do you think he's right?

Dear Sr Magdeleine,
My friend Miriam does not believe Jesus is God. What should I say to her?

Dear Sr Magdeleine,
In our town, people of different religions sometimes fight. I don't think this is right for Christians. What do you think?

Activities

1. Pretend you are Sr Magdeleine

   Choose one of the letters to answer.

   Select information from page 90 to use in your reply.

2. Think of a question about another religion that you would like to ask.

   Type your question and place it on the classroom 'Questions Display Board' or in a question box.

3. Choose one thing that you know to be part of the Christian Faith and explain it to someone of another faith.

   You can present your answer as a poster or a talk.

Research

4. Draw a Venn diagram to compare and contrast the beliefs of Christianity and one other religion.

   (a) What is unique to Christianity?

   (b) What does Christianity have in common with the other religion?

   (c) What is unique to the other religion?

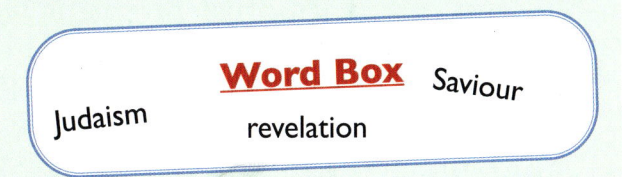

Word Box
Judaism   revelation   Saviour

Judaism and Christianity

> Know that Christianity comes from Judaism

Judaism is the faith of the Jewish people, the people chosen by God. Some great people in Judaism are Abraham, Moses, King David and the Prophets. Jesus and the twelve disciples were Jews and Christianity comes from Judaism. Christianity is the faith of those who believe that Jesus is the Son of God and the Saviour of the whole world.

King David - one of the great figures of Judaism

The roots of Christianity are in Judaism. The name 'Jesus' was a common Jewish name. It means 'God saves'.

We could say that Jews are, 'religiously speaking', the older brothers and sisters of Christians.

In fact, 2000 years ago when the Christian Church was born, people living in that area thought Christians were another type of Jew.

However, Christians are not Jews. Christianity began with Jesus and Jews do not believe that Jesus is the Son of God.

Activities

1. Look at the questions below and try to match them with the correct answers.

The most important person in Christianity is Jesus. Who is Jesus and where did he come from?	The Apostles were all born in and around Galilee. They were brought up as Jews.
The most important worship in the Church is the Mass. What is the Mass and where did it come from?	Mary lived in the village of Nazareth in Galilee. She was born and brought up as a Jewish woman.
The leaders of the early Church were the Apostles. Who were the Apostles and where did they come from?	The Old Testament was almost all written in Hebrew, the religious language of the Jews. God inspired Jewish writers to write it.
The greatest saint in the Catholic Church is Mary. Who was Mary and where did she come from?	Jesus was born a Jew in Bethlehem 2000 years ago. His relatives and neighbours in Nazareth were all Jewish.
The first part of the Christian Bible is the Old Testament. What is the Old Testament and where did it come from?	The Mass brings together two kinds of Jewish worship. These are synagogue worship and Temple worship.

Research

2. Choose one world religion and make a booklet to explain the following:

(a) Who was the key figure in it?

(b) What are the followers called?

(c) What are the most important beliefs?

(d) Where do the people worship?

(e) How should their beliefs affect the way they behave?

(f) Something else you find interesting in the religion.

(g) Add something important that would help others to understand this faith.

Glossary

Absolution - In the Sacrament of Reconciliation when the priest, in the place of Jesus, forgives your sins

Abuse - Use in a harmful way

Adultery - Break your marriage promises

Apostles - The twelve disciples who were close to Jesus

Ascension - When Jesus was taken up to heaven

Assumption - When Our Lady was taken up to heaven

Baptism - Sacrament bringing someone into the family of God

Belief - Faith, trust, confidence that something is true

Bidding prayers - Prayers asking God for something

Blessed Sacrament - Jesus in the form of a consecrated host in the tabernacle

Canonize - When the Church makes someone who has died a saint

Compassion - Tenderness, understanding

Conceited - To think you are much better than anyone else

Confession - In the Sacrament of Reconciliation when you tell the priest your sins

Conscience - Sense of what is right and wrong in your thoughts and actions

Contemplation - When we think about Jesus and pray to him in silence

Contrition - Sorrow

Covenant - A very important promise

Covet - To want something for yourself

Deliver - To save, to help escape

Desire - To really want something

Disciples - The followers of Jesus

Dominate - To be bossy

Dominion - Power and control

Endure - To put up with something

Eucharist - The Mass, from a Greek word meaning 'to give thanks'

False witness - To say untrue things about someone

Fast - Giving up something you like

Forgiveness - Pardon

Grace - A help or gift which comes from God

Hallowed - Holy or sacred

Holy Communion - The bread and wine changed into the body and blood of Jesus

Honour - To show respect and love

Hypocrite - Someone who pretends to be better than they really are

Idols - Things people worship as gods

Image and likeness - Resembling, looking or being like

Immortal soul - The invisible part of you which is not your body, that lives forever

Incarnation - When God truly became a man

Judaism - The faith of Israel

Kingdom of God - When God comes to live and rule in our lives and the world

Lord's day - Sunday

Mass - The Sacrament of the Eucharist

Meditation - When we read scripture and think about it

Missionary - Someone sent to bring the good news of Jesus

Mysteries - Parts of the life of Jesus and Mary which we think about when we pray the Rosary

Original grace - The special friendship we originally had with God

Original sin - Selfish behaviour we have inherited from Adam and Eve

Pagan - Someone not baptised, who may believe in other gods

Pardon - Forgiveness

Penance - Something to make up for the damage done by sin

Petition - An 'asking' prayer

Queen of Heaven - Title given to Mary

Rabbuni - Teacher

Reconciliation - The sacrament we receive when we confess and receive forgiveness for our sins

Refugee - Someone forced to leave their country

Repent - To be sorry for the wrong things you have done and to want God's forgiveness

Respect - To admire, honour

Resurrection - When Jesus, who had died, was raised up to new life

Revelation - How God showed himself to Israel

Revenge - Getting your own back

Sabbath - The holy day when Jews rest from work and bless God (Saturday)

Sacrament - A very important gift from Jesus, when we receive special help and grace

Saint - Holy person who loves God

Saviour - A name given to Jesus, because he died and rose again to 'save' everyone from sin and death

Sin - Offence against God, when we fail to love

Spiritual - To do with your religion, and your spirit, not just your body

Steward - Someone who looks after something

Subdue - To bring under control

Synagogue - A place of worship and learning for Jewish people

Temple - Place of religious worship

Temptation - Thoughts that lead us to behave wrongly if we give in to them

Ten Commandments - Ten rules for living a good life given by God to Moses and the people of Israel

Tiberias - A lake in Gallilee, where Jesus lived

Tomb - Where someone is buried

Trespasses - Wrong things we do

Turban - Headress worn by men

Venial sins - Sins that weaken our freindship with God

Vocal prayer - Praying aloud

Vulnerable - Weak, easily hurt

Womb - The place in the mother where a baby grows

Workhouse - Where poor people were forced to work

Worship - To adore, respect, praise

Nihil obstat: Father Anton Cowan - Censor
Imprimatur: Rt Rev Alan Hopes, V.G.
Auxiliary Bishop in Westminster
Westminster, 22 February 2003
Feast of Chair of St Peter

The Nihil obstat *and* Imprimatur *are a declaration that the book or pamphlet is considered to be free from doctrinal or moral error. It is not implied that those who have granted the* Nihil obstat *and the* Imprimatur *agree with the contents, opinions or statements expressed.*

Design, compilation and format copyright © 2003 The Incorporated Catholic Truth Society.
Text copyright © 2003 Marcellina Cooney.
Published 2003 by The Incorporated Catholic Truth Society,
40-46 Harleyford Road,
London SE11 5AY
Tel: 020 7640 0042   Fax: 020 7640 0046
website: www.cts-online.org.uk

ISBN: 978 1 86082 195 0
Designed and Produced by: The Catholic Truth Society/Stephen Campbell.
Picture research: The Catholic Truth Society/Pierpaolo Finaldi.
Front cover: *The Resurrection* © Pete Smith/ Beehive Illustration.
Printed by: The Magazine Printing Company plc - www.magprint.co.uk

Acknowledgments
Considerable thanks are due to the teachers in the following schools who contributed to the development of this Pupil Book 5 by way of advice, editorial review and comment. The Way, the Truth and the Life Series has been a collaborative exercise: kind thanks are expressed in particular to the following schools: Farleigh School, Andover; Notre Dame School, Greenwich; Our Lady of Lourdes School, Barnet; Sacred Heart School, Barnet; St Teresa's School, Harrow; St Vincent's School, Barnet; Presentation College, Reading.

Editorial Team
Louise McKenna, Amette Ley, Elizabeth Redmond, Anthony O'Rourke, Laura Lamb,
Clare Watkins and Marcellina Cooney.

Professional Curriculum Adviser
Margaret Cooling

Theological Adviser
Mgr Michael Keegan

Illustrations: © Dave Thompson, © Kate Sheppard, © Peter Smith, © Adrian Barclay, © Darrell Warner/ Beehive Illustration; © Sally Launder, © Liz Macintosh / Linda Rogers Associates.

Permission credits: Photography: © Lorenzo Lees: pages: 5, 10, 38, 62, 68. © Getty Images. Pages: 4, 34, 59, 71, 80, 81, 86, 87. Page 7: © Royalty-Free/CORBIS. Page 10 compiled from images courtesy of photodisc and Lorenzo Lees. Page 13: The Expulsion of Adam and Eve from Paradise (oil on canvas) by Francesco Curradi (1570-1649), Giraudon / Bridgeman Art Library. Page 33: © Images.com/CORBIS. Page 32: The Virgin and Child in a Landscape (oil on poplar panel) by Bernardino Luini (c.1480-1532), Wallace Collection, London, UK / Bridgeman Art Library. Page 34 © PA Photos. Page 43: St. Nicholas Distributes his Three Bags of Gold, c. 1705 (oil on canvas) by Giovanni Antonio Pucci (1679-c.1736), Oratorio de San Niccolo, Vernio, Tuscany, Italy / Bridgeman Art Library. Page 56: © Christopher Le Brun Courtesy of Marlborough Fine Arts. Page 74: Agony in the Garden by Giovanni Bellini (c.1430-1516), National Gallery, London, UK / Bridgeman Art Library. Page 78: The Ascension (vellum) by Jean Fouquet (c.1420-80), Musee Conde, Chantilly, France / Bridgeman Art Library, The Coronation of the Virgin (detail) by Giusto de'Menabuoi, courtesy of the Trustees, The National Gallery, London. Page 82: © Chris Lisle/CORBIS. Page 87: © Dave Bartruff/CORBIS, © Hanan Isachar/CORBIS, *The Chair of St Peter*, detail of the stained glass window behind, 1665, by Giovanni Bernini (1598-1680), St Peter's, Vatican, Rome, Italy/Bridgeman Art Library. Page 88: © John-Marshall Mantel/CORBIS, © James Marshall/CORBIS. (For those images or texts for which we have been unable to trace the copyright holder, the Publisher would be grateful to receive any information as to their identity).